W9-BGM-290

BRAND ECHONOMICS: BUILDING A MESSAGE THAT MATTERS

BRAND ECHONOMICS™

Building a Message That Matters

JEFF BRADY

Brand Echonomics: Building a Message That Matters
©2013 by Anchorman Media LLC

ALL RIGHTS RESERVED, including the right of reproduction in whole or in part in any form without prior written permission, except in the case of brief quotations embodied in critical reviews and certain other noncommercial uses permitted by copyright law. Contact the publisher for permission requests.

Book ordering: special discounts are available for quantity sales by corporations, associations and other public entities. Contact the publisher for more details.

Published by Inspire On Purpose™
909 Lake Carolyn Parkway, Suite 300
Irving, Texas 75039
Toll Free Phone 888-403-2727
The Platform Publisher™
www.inspireonpurpose.com

Cover Design © John Mattos 2012

Printed in the United States of America
Library of Congress Control Number: 2012939750

ISBN 10: 0982562225
ISBN 13: 978-0-9825622-2-2

CONTACT JEFF BRADY
To book Jeff for corporate speaking events call
(972) 506 0202
For more information visit
www.jeffbradyspeaks.com

Dedicated to Sam H. Brady

Outdoorsman, Entrepreneur, Philanthropist, Storyteller,
Historian, Humorist and World-Class Father

Best Echo Ever

CONTENTS

SECRETS OF A RECOVERING JOURNALIST

R EALLY?
        Do we really need another book about branding, media, and marketing?

Nope.

We need a completely different approach. A new formula. A paradigm shift. Something from the perspective of a newsroom scribe. An insider.

Why?

In this convoluted and crowded media marketplace, you'd better have an amazingly good, super-creative, relevant, never-before-told story to convey, or you'll be trampled and forgotten. Believe me. Over the past few decades as a TV news guy, I've done my share of trampling and I know how quickly and completely it happens. I wrote this book to help you *tell a better story* and *leverage media* to *reach the right audience.* That's the point.

Reading this book will not make you any more money. If, however, you APPLY the principles in this book, you'll be well on your way to a better payday.

Maybe you're an entrepreneur, like me. You think you have a better product or service, or at least a better way to offer something wonderful to the world. A sweet concept the global community has been waiting to enjoy. Or, perhaps you just like the idea of doing things yourself.

Maybe you were downsized in the "Great Recession" of 2009, 2010, or 2011 and you're starting over by forming a small business.

Maybe you're the chief marketing officer of a small, medium, or major business and you're frustrated by the ineffectiveness of your current ad or PR campaign. The audience is scattered and so is the ROI (return on investment).

Or maybe you're in business development for a successful non-profit but are finding the donors and their dollars harder to reach. With government resources also drying up, you need to find a new tool to tap into deep pockets.

Or maybe you just graduated from college or finished that MBA and you've had a hard time landing your first job, so you've decided to hang out the shingle as a freelancer, a consultant, or a "project specialist."

Regardless of your goal, you have some work to do. You have a brand message to build—a value pitch to relate to the world. In the 1950s, this was called the "Unique Selling Proposition." Later, this effort to make average products stand out on the grocery shelf was called a "Value Proposition." Now, brands have to do much more than simply stand out. Brands have always been required to reach the right audience and resonate, but today, that's just the beginning.

Most successful modern brands should also:

(a) Solve an important, urgent problem,

(b) Tap an emotional trigger, almost a spiritual nerve,

(c) Prove to be a good steward of the community by serving a larger, selfless cause, and

(d) Most importantly, each brand should involve a memorable story, a story so powerful that it grows legs.

Sound intimidating? Don't worry. As you are doubtless aware, we live in an era of massive media migration. The old giants (the dinosaurs) of big media are still lumbering about, but they don't command the same massive audiences, and many new media platforms have emerged. These are powerful little dynamos, some of which are attracting enormous crowds. Meanwhile, the audience is more sophisticated and suspicious than ever before. We've all become jaded media consumers. So how does anyone build a brand in this evolutionary, disruptive media jungle?

Glad you asked.

Maybe you've already explored the use of TV commercials or seen the glossy proposals for TV ad campaigns and their reach but found the cost, even in smaller local markets, staggering. Maybe you've run a series of print ads in a local or municipal newspaper, but with dismal ROI. Maybe you've already created a Facebook fan page, but have yet to see it drive real business, and you're wondering if it's an appropriate place for your corporate logo in the first place. Or maybe you've been to a trendy seminar or a conference by a new media guru or author but found that the advice didn't prove worthwhile just a few days later.

If you fall into any of the above marketing categories and you're wondering how to develop and grow a brand that tells the right story to the right audience, this little book is for you.

Over the course of the next several pages, I'd like to offer my services as your media quarterback, branding navigator, recovering journalist, or whatever title fits, because I'm right there in the middle of the media migration myself.

I'm one of those old-school mass-media dinosaurs—but I'm evolving right along with the technology. I'm not a new media expert, social media czar, or coach—just a journalist with his ear to the ground, listening to the roar of change and seeing how media consumption habits are evolving. Of this I am certain: technologies will surely come and go, but some of the most profound principles of communication will not. That's the basis of Brand Echonomics, a term we've coined to describe the process of building a brand message that resonates, which is the basis of this book.

I retired from TV news at the age of forty-six; while I was in the catbird seat of broadcast journalism. I had a plum job in the fifth-largest media market in the United States, anchoring the 5 p.m. newscast among a heralded team of top-shelf journalists and friends. But I saw the media landscape evolving around me and wanted to dive in headfirst instead of waiting for the brontosaurus to evolve.

The result is a how-to book told from the perspective of a recovering journalist on how to build a great brand by telling a great story. Or, better yet, I hope it inspires a great story to be told about you and your company. That's the essence of what I call Brand Echonomics: the BRAND ECHO is what remains after your pitch and your product have left the room, and it goes beyond the concept of a brand promise. Way beyond.

In the next few pages, I will unpack what I've seen amid the evolving media landscape and leave you with a working knowledge of brand-building principles for the new era, whether you end up with a campaign playing out before millions during the Super Bowl or before a few dozen who read your blog.

I'll apologize in advance that many of my references are based in Dallas. Mea Culpa. I'm a product of my environment.

In addition, you may have noticed that my writing is clipped and concise. Even abrupt. For that, I'll blame a career in broadcasting. I don't have a ghostwriter or a partner who prefers long-hand or long sentences. Consider this a conversation more than a textbook.

Brand Echonomics: Building a Message That Matters is about recruiting an army of advocates by delivering value and a script that delighted clients are eager to share on any and every media platform.

Also, as a journalist, I like to get to the point. And, as a broadcast journalist, I'm even more committed to getting from Point A to Point B as quickly as possible. That's especially true because I know how time-challenged we have all become. So, the most crucial concepts of each chapter are summarized under each chapter heading. They provide the basic concepts to revitalize your brand message and help trigger a monster media campaign.

I am here to serve you. I believe there's a little "journalist DNA" in everyone, just itching to find a great story that touches a nerve and makes a difference. I am here to help you find that story and make that difference.

THE INVISIBILITY ISSUE

Drum roll, Please...

> Most companies, even the successful ones, are virtually invisible on the commercial landscape because the owners and brand stewards don't understand their clients well enough to craft messages that resonate.

The first Big Secret is this: Most brands are invisible.

Most brand messages do NOT matter. They don't register. They don't resonate. They don't stick. This isn't good news, and yet it's oddly empowering once you understand the opportunity. Regardless of your product, company, industry, or service, you have a nearly blank canvass on which to create your brand message because your competitors have no enduring Brand Identity. At the same time, more people than ever need your help. More people are searching the media landscape, where information is accessible like never before and data is churned out at unparalleled levels. Customers, clients and consumers are voracious for solutions to a host of problems. From real estate to retail, healthcare to hair salons, I challenge anyone to name more than a few powerful brands in a single industry.

Brands that solve problems and tell great stories succeed. Brands that don't meet a need or don't communicate usually die. Pretty simple. But you may be surprised at the litany of products and services that fail annually because they miss the mark on both fronts. That means the world needs all those things that can make your brand unique: value, design, efficiency, economy, ergonomics, taste, size, or whatever.

Even somewhat effective companies are often invisible because they don't impact people's lives or make a difference, so consequently there's no story. There's no 'never-before' competitive edge that triggers amazement. Like Eleanor Rigby in the iconic old Beatles' song who was "buried along with her name," they come and go with no footprints, little more than logos and headers on stacks of stationary.

The solution? Sure, make an impressive promise that helps a lot of people, and then keep the promise. We've heard it before: *the power of the promise.* But what else?

BIG SECRET NUMBER TWO: BRAND ECHONOMICS GOES BEYOND THE PROMISE.

We know that a brand promise is made between the merchant and the buyer, and the better you honor the promise, the more your business prospers. But a Brand Echo is more.

Brand Echonomics is the study and practice of generating a commercial ripple that travels organically (horizontally and virally) between consumers. A Brand Echo is a promise that travels laterally, automatically and independently—consumer to consumer. It's not a promise from a distant merchant, but a Personal Stamp of Approval.

Word of Mouth 3.0.

First, the basics:

1. Brands matter because they drive revenue by eliciting emotional reactions. Think of some successful luxury brands: DeBeers, Mont Blanc, Jaguar. You WANT that stamp of legendary quality these brands represent. Because emotion is involved and often out-weighs every other factor, consumers pay more for brands that have some perceived exceptional value. Is the price differential commensurate with the difference in quality? Debatable. Yet they always measure up to the expectation, otherwise the brand is eroded. Think of some top economy brands: Chevy, Patron, McDonalds, Budweiser and Amazon. Are these products intrinsically better than their competitors? That's also debatable. But the brands are superstars because they trigger emotion. They elicit an emotional response, and so each brand's allure persists.

2. The OLD Set of P's. In 1960, a marketing professor at Michigan State University, E. Jerome McCarthy, proposed the "Four P" model of marketing: Product, Price, Promotion and Place. Build a great bicycle, price it right, promote it the right way, get it placed in the right stores, and you'll make money, he said. Understand the ideal "mix" of these four "P" components, and your efforts will succeed. Ever since, marketing students have analyzed and lionized the formula. No seasoned business-person would write a business plan without including a section on marketing that addresses these four topics.

9

3. Design. This is the logo, color, and font department. This stuff matters because you're talking about the graphic representation of your brand. And it should somehow translate your identity into a visual form. Think of the John Deere, Tiffany's and FedEx logos. Each conveys some core attribute of the company's product or services. Durability, glamour, and reliable delivery are intrinsic to the respective corporate symbol of each company, right?

4. Voice. Every piece of copy should convey the attitude, personality and priorities of the company. For Borden, maybe it's all about wholesomeness, while for GoDaddy, sassy sarcasm. For the U.S. Marine Corps, it's all about pride and patriotism: Can you make the cut to be one of "the few"? The tag line worked on me—and I signed up in college.

5. Consistency. You have to follow through. Once you've decided on the above, you have to stick to it. Otherwise, what's the point?

These principles have all worked well for decades. Now, however, a new media landscape is evolving in real time, right beneath our feet—and it demands a new set of guidelines for successful media messaging.

THE NEW SET OF P'S

In the twenty-first century, we at BMG (Brady Media Group) believe that each powerful brand will have to make an impact in one or more of what we call the New Basic P's: a great product, exceptional performance, or a higher passion.

To reach excellence, your brand must excel in one of these areas—and thereby generate a contagious message that evolves into a Brand Echo.

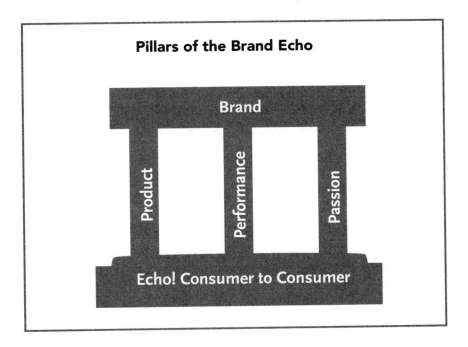

Pillars of the Brand Echo

Brand

Product

Performance

Passion

Echo! Consumer to Consumer

P IS FOR PRODUCT

Some powerful brands represent great products that are memorable strictly because of the stunning quality or durability of the tangible item. They have that 'never let you down' characteristic. Think of Craftsmen tools, Shakespeare fishing rods, Oreo cookies, Gibson guitars, Maserati sports cars, Jimmy Choo pumps, John Deere tractors, Nikon cameras, winter coats from Lands' End, or Ping golf clubs. Then there's the coffee at Café Brazil, a restaurant in Dallas. (My favorite flavor is Cinnamon Pecan. Cafe Brazil is not as well known as the rest, but the consistency of the product (coffee) keeps customers like me coming back.)

These brands first reflect detailed knowledge and understanding of the customer. A specific need is met again and again. Secondly, these brands represent the expertise of the designers who created the product—the magic mix of the center of an Oreo cookie or the precise density, heft and shape of a Craftsman hammer. They demonstrate the devotion and commitment and passion of its creators. Every time. The consistency and reliability are essential to the brand. The Big Mac is the Big Mac—with the same distinctive Thousand Island dressing—whether it's purchased at 11 a.m. in Boston, or 11 p.m. in Beaumont, Texas. There is almost always an exceptional understanding of the client and his or her expectations, and the product delivers every time.

P IS FOR PERFORMANCE

Other brands pledge exceptional performance in customer service. Think Nordstrom's department store. Ritz-Carlton Hotels. Disney World. Publix. Lexus. Cabela's. All have legendary histories of delivering extraordinary service. After hours, in the rain, for an exceptionally demanding customer who didn't deserve the attention.

More local examples of brands that offer exceptional performance include Sewell Auto Dealerships, Elliott's Hardware, and Lone Star Shipping right here in Dallas.

Each of these companies offers a similar commitment to customer service that the national brands have made famous.

Carl Sewell is arguably one of the most successful car salesmen in Texas, with fifteen dealerships across the state. A pioneer in customer satisfaction, he was the first Texas dealer named to the "Visionary Dealer" list by *Automotive News*. He even wrote a book on this topic, *Customers for Life*, in which he explains his passion for service. One example will suffice: His car dealerships will periodically send a locksmith to the airport for a customer who has flown home and found his car in the airport parking lot, only to discover he's lost his keys. The service is free. Why? Performance. Mr. Sewell has discovered that this kind of service has impact, cements the relationship, and creates customers-for-life.

Elliott's Hardware, a traditional hometown hardware shop in Dallas, has built a reputation for providing the kind of experienced home improvement know-how that the big-box home repair suppliers cannot. Elliott's deploys master carpenters and experienced plumbers on the floor to help customers make smart decisions about the products they buy. The owners understand that most customers need guidance for home repair, so they provide it. Why? Performance. It's impressive and distinct.

Lone Star Shipping is a small retail shipping and postal supply center near SMU that will safely box and ship anything anywhere, often on credit. It even offers drive-through service for harried customers who don't have time to park and walk in. The owner understands that time is precious and customers don't want to waste it standing in line. Performance. Doing what the competitor will not.

Lesson: All these merchants put a premium on knowing the customers, identifying a pain point, and a solving the problem. Remember those key points; we'll analyze that formula soon. Here's the take-away: Like these enormously successful companies, the most efficient way to build a Brand Echo is by focusing on service and putting a service mindset first. It won't require years of R and D to design the perfect hammer, just insight and performance.

P IS FOR PASSION

Brands driven by a higher passion are powerful. These businesses are known for their passionate commitment to doing whatever it takes to make a difference in the community or for a specific cause. That commitment usually aligns with the priority or belief system of both the founder and the ideal customer

For example, Patagonia supports worldwide environmental causes, Kenneth Cole supports human rights and AIDS research, and Chick-fil-A supports Christian and parenting issues.

However, I need to make a distinction between a passionate 'cause to serve' and unscrupulous "cause marketing," which often exploits the movement-of-the-moment for commercial gain, as exemplified by a well-known cola brand and polar bears.

Even more importantly, identifying and owning the passionate purpose of your business is, for many successful corporations, a core principle. It helps to focus the entire business around a central objective BEYOND cash flow. It's usually originated by the founder, and he or she uses it to energize the leadership team, whose members in turn challenge the rest of the company, which in turn amplifies the performance and sometimes even the product. Entire books and workshops are devoted to the critical importance of discovering purpose, so no need to dive deep here. However, the purpose journey is critically important and helps drive businesses that create powerful Brand Echoes.

No doubt about it.

[Warning: I'm an omnivorous reader and I'll be throwing several book references at you in the coming pages. Consider them the essential footnotes of the works cited. Cliffnotes from Jeff.]

Roy Spence, CEO of Austin ad agency GSD&M, asserts in his 2009 book It's Not What You Sell, It's What You Stand For *that companies*

often need the call of a higher passion to reach higher performance. He says, "You have to identify and articulate the purpose of the organization to have a meaningful starting point to build a brand."

Spot on.

He cites Kohler, BMW and AARP as examples of companies with whom his team has worked to help identify the "core."

In Start with Why, *author Simon Sinek puts it this way: "For a message to have real impact, to affect behavior and seed loyalty, it needs more than publicity. It needs to publicize some higher purpose, cause or belief to which those with similar values and beliefs can relate."*

Check.

And, having identified a core purpose for the business helps solidify the product, the performance, and helps identify a passion that will drive a strong Brand Echo.

A recent study by Ketchum, the noted PR and marketing agency, indicates that people are willing to change their purchasing behavior if the corporate cause aligns with their personal passions and impacts them, their community, or someone close to them. Specifically:

- "Passion for a cause is the top reason Americans evangelize a particular brand and the cause it supports, with thirty-eight percent of adults saying it's the primary reason they have written, blogged, or tweeted about a brand or cause."

- "People want cause support to be simple and easy. Forty-eight percent are most receptive to programs from which companies donate a portion of sales to a cause, and thirty-eight percent want companies to make it easy to support a cause online (e.g., become a Facebook friend)."

- "About half—four percent—of those surveyed are motivated to buy a product from a company when it makes a donation to a local school or organization, a figure that jumps to seventy percent for older adults aged sixty-five to seventy-six."

- "According to a 2011 Social Media Matters study by BlogHer, Americans are most passionate about causes supporting breast cancer initiatives (forty-four percent), animals (thirty-six percent), and children's causes (thirty-five percent)."

So what meaningful cause can your business support, and how can you help rally external support and attention toward that cause? Those were the typical questions before Brand Echonomics.

Now: Smart brand stewards are asking how to make that same cause a part of the Brand's core identity and purpose.

Then: How can those stewards help ignite a message based on the Product, Performance or Passion at the center of the Brand? A message that matters?

Branding Re-Dux.

MORE THAN A MARK

Why Do Good Brands Last Forever?

> Every brand has the potential to become legendary.
> Authenticity matters. Word of mouth is back.

Another Big Secret: This may not be pleasant to learn, but you're NOT the most important brand messenger regarding your product or service. Neither is your CMO or ad agency.

Echo: A sound heard repeatedly, often far from its source, after being reflected. (Dictionary.com)

AN ECHO is a message that lives on. It reverberates and is carried beyond its origins because of specific acoustic circumstances. It's basically a noise that goes viral. If you've been to the Grand Canyon or the rotunda of Congress, you've most likely produced an Echo yourself.

So the term "Brand Echo" represents the kind of brand message that gets traction because of the distinct, organic power of the concept—and the context in which it launched. It doesn't need to be pushed or promoted; it's contagious. Unlike the lofty Brand Promise, which is projected by the owner, manufacturer, or provider (often at great expense), the Brand Echo travels laterally from one consumer to another like a summer breeze. The echo gets repeated automatically, orally, and on numerous media platforms. It is honest, transparent, and compelling; it becomes a "trans-media" concept that inspires amazement, travels virally, and has a lasting impact. People remember it.

Promise v. Echo

Brand Promise	Brand Echo
Push Media	Pull Media
Top-Down	Lateral (Organic, Viral)
Originates with Owner	Originates with Consumer
Single Primary Media Channel	Trans-Media (Any Channel)
Expensive ($$$)	Free

"Brand Echonomics" is the study of how this happens.

The merchant no longer delivers the most important brand message. Instead, the most critical pitch, commercial, or endorsement comes from satisfied customers who want to share the news of an effective product or service with an intimate circle of friends who listen and learn from each other. Word of mouth survives as the most effective tool to build a brand—and this has never been truer than in this age of social media.

Let me repeat: even in this hyper-connected world of mobile social media, word of mouth remains the most potent platform in which to build a brand.

The Brand Echo term may be new, but the concept goes way back.

I have a ten-foot-wide antique wooden barn door in my home office. It's a massive, rectangular piece that originated in a black-smith's shop in Central Texas and has several dozen authentic cattle brands from the turn of the last century seared deeply into the wood. It's been in my family a long time, and it's a fitting metaphor for Brand Echonomics.

My Barn Door

Factoid: The act of marking livestock with fire-heated marks to identify ownership has origins in ancient times, with the use dating back to the ancient Egyptians. In English lexicon, the word "brand" originally meant anything hot or burning, such as "firebrand," a burning stick. [Source: Wikipedia]

Whether the brand owner acknowledges it or not, whether or not an investment is made in protecting its exclusive use, and regardless of the amount of attention paid to the quality and caliber of the product bearing the brand, that brand—every brand—represents a lot.

This may sound ambitious, even presumptuous. After all, brands are ubiquitous today. Almost every new car, candy bar, and drug cartel has one. Most don't involve a heartfelt promise between the business owner and the buyer, but they should. Most don't inspire an echo between buyers, either. What's there to talk about? Very few companies offer *truly* exceptional products, extraordinary customer service, or powerful causes.

But what if they did?

ABOVE ALL, BE AUTHENTIC

Fundamentally, a powerful brand symbolizes the bond made between merchant and consumer. It connotes the value, standards, success, and reach of a company. It should evoke the Product, Performance or Passion, as well as the impact on customers. And here's the key: Passionate customers (or Catalysts) become the ones communicating the message.

In addition, the more ethereal the product or service, the more important the Catalyst. That is, the less tangible the product, the more important the brand and its objective advocate. If the company builds watches, cars, or airplanes, the item at the end of the assembly line can stand alone. Rolex vs. McKinsey. Porsche vs. CNN. Which brand name produces a more tangible, concrete image? If the company provides financial or IT consulting, party planning, or TV news, the branding takes on more importance—simply because there is no physical product to carry the weight.

See?

Believe me, I know. Broadcast journalism, more than almost any other industry, is built on intangible brands. Whether served up by CBS, NBC, CNN, or Dallas-based WFAA, the brand residue can evaporate as soon as the broadcast ends. There is absolutely nothing distinct about a recitation of the facts of the day, regardless of how much a news operation pounds home the message that the story is exclusive, urgent, or late-breaking.

Consequently, every newsroom I served spent massive amounts of time and resources reminding audiences of the distinct, presumptive value of the news product we rendered. We were "Live, Local, and Late-Breaking" or "The Spirit of Texas" in every newscast. In most cases, the news content was average and routine—even a commodity. On any given night, about seventy-five percent of the entire newscast could be found elsewhere. So the branding was critical.

In the same way, many gargantuan consumer brands have spent billions over the last several decades pounding home catchy brand messages about routine products.

"Two all-beef patties…"
"Every kiss begins with…"
"You're in good hands with…"
"Good to the last…"

In the modern media landscape, however, trite jingles carry less weight. They don't mean as much and they certainly don't influence behavior like they did in the sixties, seventies, and eighties. Consumers are more savvy. They now have access to mountains of online data and make buying decisions well armed with information. Audiences expect most merchants to boast and brag, whether the assertion is true or not. In fact, audiences typically assume that advertising is bloated with subjective research and paid testimonials. That's why an honest, authentic merchant really stands out.

What an opportunity!

THE NEW WORD OF MOUTH

In addition, the only recommendations and referrals we digest today are those of close friends and family. A recent study by the Nielsen Global Trust shows that only 14% of the American public trust ads, but 78% trust consumer recommendations, even from consumers they don't know. And, with social media, word-of-mouth marketing has mushroomed into the single most cost-effective sales engine available. Because we TRUST friends, neighbors and relatives—even in a digital environment. Neighborhood opinions today now ricochet around the world.

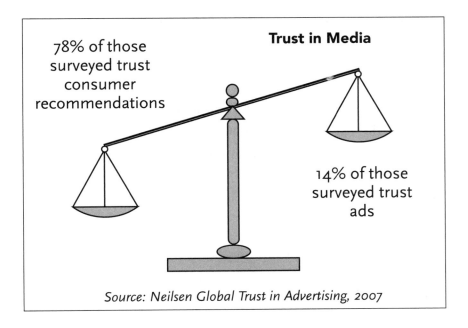

78% of those surveyed trust consumer recommendations

Trust in Media

14% of those surveyed trust ads

Source: Neilsen Global Trust in Advertising, 2007

And, it works both ways.

Poor customer service, shoddy workmanship, weak warranties, or unethical business dealings can be quickly exposed and illuminated online for a global audience. Likewise, superior products and service—and passionate causes—can get extraordinary attention. The brand story that was once a neighborhood reputation can now go global.

Examples: Crocs, *Chicken Soup for the Soul*, Life is Good T-shirts (Google any of them to see what powerful word of mouth can do!)

Technology and connectivity have changed, but human behavior has not; we're still eager to help each other with recommendations. Most of us are pleased to have experiences we can share with our closest circle of friends and family members, particularly if those experiences can entertain, teach a lesson, or convey a personal endorsement. We all yearn to engage and be affirmed as credible and valuable.

Consequently, the smartest marketers are now making it easy to spread the word with a personal recommendation (or Personal Stamp of Approval) that conveys the distinct value of the brand. They make the brand easy to remember, engineer opportunities for individual customers to have extraordinary experiences, and let the ripple of online chatter and news media coverage do what paid advertising no longer can—convey an honest, authentic affirmation about an honest and authentic brand.

Here's the goal: Let's create extraordinary experiences to foster an incredible Brand Echo for your organization and see how far it goes!

That leads me to the obvious, almost antiquated questions marketers have traditionally asked: What's the core value of your brand? What's the one thing that can and will get people talking? What can your company claim that competitors cannot? Then—what will be the Echo of your brand?

For that matter, what will be the Echo of your life's work? How will your descendants be able to:

(a) Remember your efforts,
(b) Tell your story, and
(c) Leverage the brand you're building today for financial gain?

If those topics are of interest to you, then by all means read on. We have work to do.

My goal in *Brand Echonomics* is to begin a conversation about commercial storytelling and to convey the simple process by which you can build a Brand Echo that lasts. In journalism, certain components made it into almost every story that hit the evening news. The same should be true for your brand, and I share the formula with you in the following chapters.

> Strong brands inspire organic recommendations. Customers and clients want to offer a Personal Stamp of Approval. You just need to equip them to do so.

Let's get started.

FOR DISCUSSION

Be honest: does your company have a Brand Echo?

If not, what is the one thing (product, performance or passion) that could form the foundation of a strong Brand Echo?

NOISE, NOISE, NOISE! FIGHTING MEDIA FATIGUE

> Consumers suffer from an epidemic of Information or Media Fatigue. Unsolicited media is filtered and blocked. Successful media, however, overcomes these barriers using precise context and exceptional content. Effective messaging must appeal to both hemispheres of the consumer's brain: analytic and dramatic.

Next Big Secret: Media fatigue means it is more difficult now than ever to deliver the right brand message to the right audience. Fewer people are paying attention.

In this era of media ubiquity, there is more messaging, sloganeering, advocacy, spin, hype, opinion, and banter than at any other time in human history—all of it conveyed on multiple media channels. More screens. More chirping and buzzing devices. Media clutter is the new norm, and we overdose on all of it. Every day there are more websites, more cable news chatter, more Facebook fan pages, more infomercials, and more spam. As a result, we are experiencing an attention-deficit economy. We pay attention to almost none of it.

Nobel-prize-winning economist Herbert Simon said, "A wealth of information creates a poverty of attention." So true. Too many of us are unable or unwilling to devote the time and effort required to slow down and focus. Deep, prolonged thought is extraordinarily rare these days. Ask your local psychologist.

On the other hand, media clutter is not an entirely new problem. Information overload has deep roots. Take a look at the Old Testament. Ecclesiastes 12:12 laments, "Of making many books there is no end."

Sound familiar? Our generation is different in that we have a global platform from which to harvest and on which to disseminate information. Global media sources large and small have the ability to reach out and follow us, and these rapid changes will continue. In fact, most analysts estimate that the technical evolutions of our culture will only increase in speed and scope.

Get ready...the storm is only just beginning.

As an antidote, we have erected media barriers to keep most data out.

BARRIERS

Not too long ago, the only real action on the telephone landline at the Brady home began at dinnertime, between about 5 p.m. and 7 p.m., when the telemarketers went to work. Like most Americans, Caller ID was a routine filter for us, and no one even touched the landline without first identifying the caller. Soon, the landline itself became irrelevant; we disconnected it and shut off the service. As the smart phone grows more convenient and offers ever more functions, the old land-based phone becomes more of a relic. You'll probably cancel the service soon, too.

Factoid: The Pew Research Center notes that only a decade ago, nearly all homes had a landline phone (ninety-seven percent of U.S. households in 2001). Today, just seventy-four percent of homes have a landline. Furthermore, eighty-two percent of adults now use a cell phone, up from fifty-three percent in 2000. [Source: Pew Research Center.]

In fact, all of us have more filters established now than ever before to screen out unwanted, offensive, or generic media. Opt-out websites allow us to eliminate junk mail, spam filters block unwanted emails, TiVo allows us to skip TV ads, while satellite radio offers ad-free music and news. These technology barriers are designed to keep out unwanted messaging. As the established Madison Avenue agencies launch more unsolicited and increasingly intrusive advertising campaigns, most consumers do two things: We erect more filters and shields to keep ads out and, more troublesome for advertisers, we become psychologically indifferent. We become numb—subconsciously blind to almost all unsolicited media. The key message is that unsolicited, unwanted, or irrelevant media is ignored.

BY INVITATION ONLY

It's a media battle zone.

Most messages are trampled and ignored before they are heard, seen, or read. The defensive perimeter is almost impenetrable, so the only media that really enters and impacts the lives of most consumers today is what I call BIO-Media, or, By Invitation

> Most of us are better at blocking media than at sorting and digesting it. Oddly enough, we've returned to the era of word-of-mouth marketing at a time when we are more technologically ad–vanced than ever!

Only. We voluntarily *invite* the media we want into our lives—the e-newsletters to which we subscribe, the TV programs we record, the calls we accept, the emails we recognize, the movies we request on Netflix or Vudu, or the occasional hand-written note from a friend or relative.

In light of these barriers, the question is this: does *your* media message rise to the challenge? Does it get invited to the table and/or get opened first? If not, what sort of media messages *do* get through?

Only those messages succeed that are tremendously:

- Distinct,

- Valuable, and

- Personal

So the most effective brand stewards are those who engage the potential client with the most relevant, service-oriented, problem-solving media possible. Then, to deliver the message, they often use a personal emissary: a devoted brand advocate. It's no longer enough to just be funny, or clever and creative, or even remarkable; now the message has to prove its worth. It must be powerful, pertinent, and intimate. And that's a pretty tall order.

To a degree, media has always been an opt-in transaction. We've chosen which newspaper to read and which evening newscast to watch, but earlier generations had only a fraction of the choices and control we have today. If our parents and grandparents wanted to be informed about national politics, they had limited options. If they wanted to be entertained Monday at 8:00 p.m., they had only a few channels from which to choose. Or, if a family wanted to watch the *Dick Van Dyke Show*, the opportunity occurred at the same time every Tuesday night on CBS. If they missed an episode, they were simply out of luck, but that isn't the case anymore. *Modern Family*, for example, is available on multiple digital outlets, including TiVo, HuLu, and DVD.

Today, it is increasingly common that even commercials have to be selected, or invited to the table, for viewing. Opt-in marketing is another term for BIO-Media, because if advertisers are aren't invited, they're ignored. That's why product placement, content marketing, cause marketing, and episodic, narrative commercials that convey a concise, compelling story for the viewer, the reader, the listener, or the web surfer have become more common. The new mantra is "Join the conversation; don't interrupt it." Address a common interest, concern, or problem; don't just talk about yourself. *Push media is out. "Pull" media is in.* More on that later.

I'm not proclaiming that advertising is dead, by the way. Witness the success of Google and Facebook, both billion-dollar empires built on the power of targeted digital advertising. But notice the key word: *targeted*. If it's a generic ad with little or no relevance to the current search or the topic of my recent post, I ignore it. If it's a highly pertinent ad that solves a problem I just raised, I pay attention. Obvious? Of course. But most of us don't act on this knowledge.

BECOME THE INTIMATE RESOURCE

The most important factor in achieving BIO-media status is intimacy. I discuss the Media Intimacy Index in detail in Chapter

Seven. Essentially, the index reflects the direct relationship between the brand message source and its effectiveness. The more distant (intellectually and yes, geographically) the source or the more remote the origin of the media message, the less likely it will inspire action. The more intimate the source, the more likely the recipient will listen, remember, and act.

For example, if I'm looking for a job, President Obama announcing a new jobs bill is less relevant to me than a local talk-radio interview or a Tweet from an HR director who's announcing a hundred job openings in my neighborhood. A national ad for low-interest rates on new Hondas is interesting, but not as likely to inspire me to buy as if I were to see a friend who lives a mile away bragging on Facebook about an amazing zero-interest loan for a new Accord. If I happen to see the friend in person and he gives me an enthusiastic rant about the amazing deal and takes me for a drive in the new car, even better. That's how the Brand Echo starts. Again, it begins with the Personal Stamp of Approval.

See the difference? I don't erect barriers to the media offered by my most intimate circle of friends and family. Almost everything they offer "gets through the gates," at least to a degree. As ironic as it sounds, we have now come full circle, back to an era when old-fashioned word-of-mouth marketing trumps every other media platform.

The key distinction today is that one person's "word of mouth" can circle the globe in record time. That one person might have a local following of five hundred people who read her blog or who follow her regional cooking segments on YouTube; ten percent (fifty people) of that aggregate audience could become clients of yours if she were to mention your product or service favorably online.

If, on the other hand, Matt Lauer mentions your product

or service on The Today Show, you have a massive audience of millions but a slightly lower likelihood that those viewers will identify with the process or product you offer and subsequently call your office. The show originates in New York, thousands of miles from most Americans, and the producers are bombarded with hundreds of pitches daily. The odds that you would get on the show are low in the first place, and the likelihood that your appearance will trigger an enormous response is lower. It can happen, but typically it doesn't. Instead, a satisfied hometown customer bragging about your product or service on Facebook can be MUCH more effective at driving new business, because we are living in an age when intimate mini-media often trumps mass media in both relevance and believability.

That's an important point: Mini-Media often trumps Mass Media in relevance and believability.

Honest.

In light of all this, how does Brand Echonomics help next-generation marketers and media experts "get through the gates"? By offering a highly intimate, relevant, targeted, informed, and potentially entertaining message that solves an important problem for our ideal clients. Even better, Brand Echonomics packages the message in a story that is easily remembered and forwarded. To put it another way, Brand Echonomics builds a message that matters—one that is remembered, and relayed from consumer to consumer. That is the essence of the Brand Echo. And yes, it comes in a formula. It's in Chapter Four, so wait for it.

To summarize, consumers are inundated with data but are hungry for wisdom, empathy, guidance, and intimate, relevant messaging that can help solve a problem today. They also want it close to home and free. They aren't looking for a dispassionate accountant so much as a compassionate advisor. Think in terms of a right-brain coach, not a left-brain critic.

SECRETS OF THE CALLOSUM CLUB

Interestingly, so-called "left-brain" thinkers have dominated most of the last century. Although the frequent lateralization of the brain has been criticized as over-simplified pop neurology, there is a measurable distinction between an aptitude for logic and math in the left hemisphere and one for creativity in the right. Many sociologists and futurists anticipate that we are about to enter a new era dominated by right-brain creative problem-solvers.

Dan Pink has mapped out this future in his 2006 book Whole New Mind. *He explains that Western culture has evolved through the Agrarian and Industrial Ages to the Information Age and now to the Conceptual Age. In this new era, he argues, the data-based skills valued most in the last century (accounting, computer programming, routine legal, database management, etc.) will be largely outsourced and the real economic engines of modern culture will be leveraged on so-called "right-brain" skills to include design, storytelling, dispute resolution, customer service, and entrepreneurship.*

Richard Florida presented a similar concept in his 2003 book, The Rise of the Creative Class, *which describes a sub-culture of inventors, writers, designers and entrepreneurs who (he predicts) will drive economic progress and flock to the most tolerant, educated cities in the world. While his premise has been attacked by academics for a dubious causal connection, visionary municipal leaders have largely adopted the concept. In fact, Florida's consulting firm teaches cities how to attract the creatives and a tenth anniversary edition of the book is now in print.*

I agree with the creative right-brain premise, but in my

opinion, the dominant future thinkers will belong to what I call the "Callosum Club," named after the corpus callosum in the brain, the bundle of neural fibers that connect the brain's two hemispheres. Those in the Callosum Club will be able to combine the logical and numerical left-brain with the creative and holistic right brain.

Factoid: The corpus callosum, also known as the colossal commissure, is a wide, flat bundle of neural fibers beneath the cortex at the longitudinal fissure. It connects the left and right cerebral hemispheres and facilitates inter-hemispheric communication. It is the largest white matter structure in the brain, consisting of 200-250 million contralateral axonal projections. [Source: Wikipedia]

It's already happening. Ergonomic design is already driving the sale of kitchen appliances, desktop computers, flashlights, and house paint. Creative, even theatrical, staging is driving the layout of grocery stores, convenience stores, and malls. However, retail, manufacturing and entertainment—all business sectors— still require talented bookkeeping, invoicing, payroll and contract law to be viable. Both the so-called left and right-brain skills are critical. Have we neglected the right-siders over the last few decades? Possibly. Do they deserve more affirmation? Sure.

Why does this matter to us if we're growing a brand? Successful media messages will exemplify the same characteristics. Creative logic and empathetic problem solving represent data and drama coming together at last! This is an important consideration in developing a successful Brand Echo using BIO-Media to get invited to the table. The most powerful messages of this era and the next will require elements that ignite BOTH hemispheres of the brain.

FOR DISCUSSION

How does the BIO-Media concept impact your business?

What sort of brand message would "get invited to the table" in your industry?

How can you inspire a message that is relevant to both hemispheres of the brain?

THE TRICK TO GETTING TRACTION

Make a Powerful Pledge to Serve. Then Keep It.

> Service is key. Developing a relevant and unrelenting commitment to customer service is the most efficient route to a Brand Echo. We have a culture starving for service. Knowing the client helps break down the barriers.

Big Secret: "He profits most who serves best."

On a cold Chicago day in February of 1910, Business Philosopher and Rotarian Arthur Frederick Sheldon rose to the podium at the first annual convention of the National Association of Rotary Clubs of America and declared, "... He profits most who serves best," and it stuck. It tapped a nerve. The same phrase was approved as the Rotary motto in 1911 at the second convention of Rotarians in Portland, Oregon. Sheldon's complete quote was, "Only the science of right conduct toward others pays. Business is the science of human services. He profits most who serves his fellows best."

The shortened version has been a Rotary motto ever since. No, not every Rotarian measures up to the noble standard of service, but it's there as a reminder.

Rotary Club Wheel

To this day, Rotarians are community leaders who—for the most part—surrender self to service. This goes back to dear old Dad.

My father was a founding member of the Georgetown (Texas) Rotary Club—and its first president. He devoted much of his time and best efforts toward the club and its members in the early 1960s and beyond. Why? Was he building a brand name for his local insurance agency? Of course. He was doing it, though, in the best way possible—sweat equity and service to the community in which he lived and conducted business. It's not a bad trade-off. If the service taps a real need—and stands apart—it is recognized. And the message spreads, whether on the lips of people of the twentieth or twenty-first century.

Today, the chatter might begin on a blog that generates several comments. Then it might travel to Facebook. Then people might start texting each other about it and perhaps even picking up the phone to place a call, or several hundred calls, spreading the message. Then traditional news media might pick it up and produce or publish a story about the product or service. At that point, it becomes an industry phenomenon and someone from your company or team is asked to make a presentation at the next annual convention, trade show, or conference.

In short, the message travels because of its "Value DNA." What sort of value is conveyed? People are startled, challenged, enlightened, entertained, and intrigued in a new and compelling way.

"What? A company in Round Rock, Texas, will make a custom computer based on my specific requirements?" (Promising an amazing process.)

"Huh? A teapot full of saltwater can actually cure my sinus headache?" (Promising an amazing product and a devoutly desired result.)

"Are you kidding? An airline held a loaded plane at the gate so one man could get home in time to see his two-year-old grandson in the ICU?" (Promising amazing customer service.)

Yes. Yes. And yes. All three concepts were remarkable in the not-too-distant past.

All three triggered a Brand Echo, an organic message that challenged the traditional, conventional, boring status quo. These messages spread with little or no advertising.

In the first example, Dell Computers tapped enormous pent-up demand in the PC industry by customizing the manufacture and delivery of home computers. People wanted tailored computers!

For Americans, the Neti Pot sounded like voodoo medicine at first. People were actually pouring warm salt water from a small ceramic pot up one nostril and out the other to clear sinus passages? Bizarre. But when featured on Oprah, the device was a nation-wide sensation. People needed to clear out stuffy sinuses, and this thing worked!

When Southwest Airlines held a plane packed with passengers at LAX so that one harried grandfather could make his flight home to see a grandson who was on life support in a Denver hospital, the story went around the world in a matter of hours. It started in a travel blog and ended up on every network in the U.S., as well as on many in Europe and Asia. People were dumbfounded (and then thrilled) to discover an airline that cared!

The power of a profound concept that serves a need or touches a nerve—or both—is undeniable. As French poet Victor Hugo said, "An invasion of armies can be resisted, but not an idea whose time has come."

Factoid: Victor Hugo was a French poet, playwright, novelist, essayist, statesman, and human rights activist. Hugo is sometimes identified as the greatest French poet. His best-known works are the novels Les Miserables *and* The Hunchback of Notre Dame. *[Source: Wikipedia]*

We trademarked the term Brand Echonomics to describe this pseudo-field of study. It's a nickname, really, for a big movement. What are the conditions in which a powerful, pertinent brand experience of 'service above self' can be created? Then, how is it described by customers and clients, and how is it distributed organically and consumed by millions? That process is really the point of this book.

Anne Handley is the chief content officer for MarketingProfs. In her 2007 book Content Rules, *she says, "The companies that understand that SERVING is the new SELLING will be the ones that land new customers!"*

Exactly.

PINPOINT THE ITCH

The premise is that, to evolve into a Brand Echo, the brand promise must be remarkable, *and* distinctly useful, *and* touch a raw nerve. It must trigger perpetual endorsements from an endless supply of voices.

As I mentioned in the last chapter, remarkable alone isn't enough anymore (apologies to Seth Godin). A circus at city hall is remarkable. A warehouse fire is remarkable. A purple squirrel on a tiny bicycle is remarkable. All will most likely make the evening news, but then be quickly forgotten.

Developing a Brand Echo requires a higher standard than simply being remarkable; it requires a deep knowledge of the industry, an ability to service the client's Number One need, and even better, an ability to inspire a customer or client (a Catalyst) to spread the word. If you can do all three on a consistent basis, you've got a Brand Echo to rattle the world.

Take my cousin, Nancy Upton. Google her name and you will find a case study in Brand Echonomics. She tackled a monster U.S apparel company and its condescending approach to plus-sized women with an "in-your-face" spoof on Facebook.

Basically, American Apparel launched a trite, poorly planned contest on social media soliciting plus-sized women to submit photos in an online contest to select a new model. Nancy played by the rules and submitted photos of herself that were an obvious and artistic tirade against fashion and clothing companies that pander to larger women. She won the online voting hands-down, but American Apparel denied her the title, which triggered a firestorm of support for her and animosity toward American Apparel. People talked, Tweeted, and repeated her story everywhere. It went viral with no massive PR campaign at all.

After hundreds of blistering attacks in social media and almost as many interviews in traditional media outlets, including *The Huffington Post*, *Time*, and The Today Show, American Apparel made amends. Nancy touched a nerve in a clever, even remarkable, way and created an instant Brand Echo.

How could you elicit that same kind of viral interest?

SHEER UNMATCHED VALUE

Imagine your customers being dumbfounded by the sheer unmatched value of your product or service. Think of the power of making people see that your company actually understands a chronic, serious need in the community and offers something of profound value that the competitors do not. Imagine that your corporation, small business or nonprofit actually matches or (gasp!) exceeds expectations. What would this product or service look like, what would the experience be for the customer, and what would the impact be?

What sort of Echo would emerge?

The problem in today's business culture is that almost all business owners or proponents *think* they have a brand message of this caliber, and almost none do. Consequently, they spend obscene amounts of money on marketing, advertising, and PR projects to proclaim a message that carries no weight. They are largely invisible because they are irrelevant. If your tagline contains the words "Quality," "Trust," or "Value," you're saying the same thing virtually every other merchant in America is saying, regardless of the industry. It's a boring, banal message.

Instead, describe the quality, explain the trust, offer a concrete example of the value embodied, and be succinct. Or—even better—provide an experience in which the customer encounters the quality, trust-worthiness and value, and is then equipped to deliver the message herself.

The number of wasted story pitches newsrooms receive supports this claim. Whether by Twitter, email, snail mail, or voicemail, nine of the ten story ideas submitted to journalists are centered on ordinary products or services served up in ordinary ways under ordinary circumstances. That is, rather than being newsworthy, they are boring. Ask any major-market journalist how many emails go unanswered each day simply because they do not deserve a response.

The answer is hundreds. If you don't have a powerful Brand Echo, your pitch is most likely one that ends in the delete file.

Factoid: PR Newswire and Marketwire recently responded to a Twitter survey by Journalistics—regarding the number of press releases distributed each day. Both agencies replied with approximately one thousand. Think about it. There are easily a dozen press release agencies submitting pitches daily. If the average reporter only gets one percent of those releases, that equates to about seven or eight hundred per week. And that's a lot of work. [Source: Journalistics]

Tip from the old reporter's notebook: Before calling any reporter anywhere to pitch a business-related news story, ask yourself three questions:

1. Can you truthfully say this has *never* been done before? At least, not in *this* way or in *this* town?

2. Does it *affect* more than a thousand people (approximately)? Or, does it affect *one* person to such a profound degree that thousands could identify with the circumstances?

3. Does it have *broad implications* to tap an unmet need among a wide constituency? (That is, would someone who is not directly affected care?)

Positively answering two of these three questions might constitute a valid news story, but believe me, if none of the above apply, *it ain't news!* Save the call and don't distribute the drab press release. No one will read it, much less offer news coverage. On the other hand, it is absolutely true that the best stories sell themselves. If a story has real news merit it typically gets coverage without much of a push.

TIME TO REVIEW

In the first section, we considered three key areas in which brands can make powerful promises. Remember? They are the three Ps: a great product, exceptional performance, or a higher passion. Anyone can make a promise, hire an ad agency to organize the media buy, write a snappy tag line and launch the new product line. But an Echo requires more. Establishing a strong reputation in any one of these areas can trigger a Brand Echo, but the quickest and most economical means for doing so is by offering exceptional performance. Quite simply, over-deliver extreme customer service and a Brand Echo will occur.

Whether you are manufacturing cars or can openers, if you are prepared to invest heavily in R and D, then perhaps you can create a remarkable product that generates an Echo. Sir James Dyson did it in 1992. In fact, his iconic products now represent twenty-three percent of the four-billion-dollar U.S. vacuum-cleaner market. That's great Brand Echo.

If you have a profound commitment to some charitable cause and you know it resonates with the commercial demographic you want to reach, perhaps the Echo will be generated by a public pledge to make a difference. Blake Mycoskie did it in 2006 when he founded TOMS Shoes to help provide shoes to low-income Argentinian kids. Since then, the for-profit company has sold more than two million pairs of shoes and clears at least $100 million annually. Not a bad business model.

In Start with Why, *Simon Sinek writes, "We are drawn to leaders and organizations who are good at communicating what they believe. Their ability to make us feel like we belong, to make us feel special, safe and not alone is part of what gives them the ability to inspire us. Those whom we consider great leaders all have an ability to draw us close and to command our loyalty."*

However, my belief is that the most cost-effective and immediate means of developing a powerful Brand Echo is through extraordinary customer service. Identify the pain point and solve it with service, if possible. Many prominent companies have grown brand messages with strong commitments to customer service: USAA, Cabela's, Publix, Southwest Airlines, Apple, Nordstrom, Ritz-Carlton, Four Seasons, Lexus and Ace Hardware are all good examples.

But by any measure, the vast majority of companies have not even begun to create Brand Echoes with extraordinary service. It is a simple solution that few companies pursue.

To recap, the best process of triggering a powerful Brand Echo is usually an effort to become more customer-oriented and then to deliver a truly amazing product, great performance or a passionate cause, not tricking or begging the media to cover a lame concept. My conviction, however, is that the most powerful and permanent Brand Echoes are created in the PERFORMANCE category by delivering exceptional customer service.

To begin building a powerful Brand Echo, consider the following series of questions:

1. How distinct is your current message? Is it similar to your competitors?

2. What extreme service can you promise that your customers crave—one that your competitors cannot or will not deliver?

3. How can you serve up the story/message in a way that customers will remember and share? How can you deliver a remarkable experience, which will trigger an Echo?

In short, what is your commitment? What is the real UVP, or *unique value proposition*, that will resonate with your clients and that will make your product or service visible? What is the blended "passionate purpose" message that will get your brand invited to the table? How can you amplify your service to earn an Echo?

Outrageous (but groundless) marketing campaigns and clever (but irrelevant) ads are usually ignored today. It really doesn't matter how many billboards you rent, and a funny radio spot only lasts about thirty seconds.

SERVICE REMAINS IN STYLE

Service, on the other hand, never goes out of style.

At the risk of being redundant, I believe the most cost-effective means of developing a strong Brand Echo is by investing in radical customer service and making that approach a part of your business model.

Amaze friends, vendors, and customers with your commitment to provide exceptional service, one client at a time. Are any of your competitors known for providing amazing customer service? If not, then why not? Ask yourself what amazing customer service would mean in your industry or for your clients. Brands are built in the trenches, where customers come into contact with your company in personal exchanges. What will that experience be? Provide an experience that knows no comparison.

> Stand out by providing service. It's easier, quicker, and more doable than "building a better mousetrap." Few others are doing it, and customers crave it!

Joseph Pine and James Gilmore in their 1999 bestseller The Experience Economy *note that, "The staging of experiences must be pursued as a distinct form of economic output."*

Give your customers an experience to talk about. What level of service would convert every client into a Catalyst for your brand? How can you provide this level of service consistently and reliably? An occasional act of customer service heroism is laudable, but not enough to grow a brand. Make the "wow factor" a repeatable, measurable business practice. Make it powerful enough to trigger a Brand Echo heard 'round the world.

FOR DISCUSSION

What can you offer that no one else in your industry would even consider?

What do you pledge?

How can you create an experience that inspires an Echo?

THE TALKING STICK OF THE TWENTY-FIRST CENTURY

The One Thing Our Culture Craves

> The best communicators are storytellers. The best brands create such powerful user/client experiences that stories are created automatically and the storytellers share them.

"Why was Solomon recognized as the wisest man in the world? Because he knew more stories (Proverbs) than anyone else. Scratch the surface in a typical boardroom and we're all just cavemen with briefcases, hungry for a wise person to tell us stories."
— Alan Kay, Vice President, Walt Disney

Next Big Secret: Data can tell, but stories sell.

Everyone wants a story to tell, and everyone can remember a great story. Powerful stories become legends that teach us powerful lessons, especially those stories of individuals who pushed beyond mediocrity to win a battle, overcome the odds, or serve others on an extraordinary level. Even if the story doesn't rise to the level of a legend, it is memorable if it touches a nerve in the audience. Think of the teacher who goes beyond what is expected to make a difference in the classroom, the CPA who saves you several thousand dollars on your personal return, the waiter who provides an amazing dining experience, or the singer who really belts out a piece of her soul onstage. If you are the recipient of any of these services, you will likely talk about it. You will have a story to tell.

Forge an amazing story, and you will create an aura that people want to share. When you exceed expectations, or when people are awestruck, they want to share it with others, and they do so by telling stories. The story is remembered and spreads virally. And the more amazing the story, the farther it spreads. Like physics, the more emotionally-charged the story, the more energy it has to travel. A purposeful person who renders a service with passion will impress the client every time.

In other words, *purpose* plus *passion* results in *wow*, and the 'wow' inspires a customer to become an advocate or a Catalyst. The problem is, most marketers and advertisers tell the wrong story by keeping the focus on themselves. In other words, it's "all about them." Instead, the focus should be on the customer/ client/patient whose life is improved because of the encounter. That EXPERIENCE is the key to the story that triggers the Echo. Get it?

When told properly, that story drives everything. It plays on every channel. The better the story, the more likely it will go viral. As a journalist, I can tell you how to create this story.

The following four chapters do exactly that.

BRAIN-OLOGY 101

Intellectually, We Are Still Neanderthals

> Use the Brand Echo formula to tell a memorable story:
> (C + P + Y = Story) x Ct = Brand Echo.

Next Big Secret:
Every successful story follows an ancient formula.

"Tell me a story, Daddy." My daughter demands it every night when she's bathed and ready for bed. She's making an ancient request.

We all listen and learn from stories. In fact, neurologists believe we learn most of what we know through storytelling. It has been this way for a long, long time. We can't help it. We perk up, pay attention, perceive meaning, and propagate wisdom by way of stories. Simply put, we are hard-wired to absorb and repeat stories.

Factoid: Memory experts remember long sequences of numbers or names by connecting the dots with a narrative sequence of mental images that tell a story. We pass social norms and historical wisdom from one

generation to the next by telling stories. All great life lessons are tradi-
tionally conveyed in story form. Examples are countless, and they are
everywhere. The Epic of Gilgamesh. Aesop's Fables. The Just-so Stories
by Rudyard Kipling. The Tales of Paul Bunyan, John Henry and Uncle
Remus. [Source: BrainTraining101.com]

THE TALKING STICK

In Native American culture, when the braves and chiefs gathered
for tribal council, they had no Roberts Rules of Order to guide
parliamentary procedure. Instead, they often used the "talking
stick," an ornate wooden totem decorated with feathers and stones,
to help govern the crowd. The one who held the talking stick had
the floor to speak. All others had to wait their turn.

The Talking Stick

Mammaw, Pop and baby Jeff

My grandfather—a rural mailman in Georgetown, Texas—was also an amateur historian, student of Native American culture and a talented whittler. He could carve a cedar branch into almost any wooden implement. As a joke, he once carved a "talking stick" to help calm the clamor at our boisterous family reunions. (I grew up in a family of big talkers. Imagine that!)

We need a talking stick for the twenty-first century just to cut through the clutter, be heard, and capture the attention of an audience above the din and clamor of the modern media circus. Every Facebook post, YouTube video, blog entry, tweet, billboard, web article, TV program, email, and hi-definition monitor is competing for the attention of your next client. You need something to help you stand out. Even Coke needs something to help it stand out.

The solution is the story—the deceptively simple story. This simple, yet sophisticated messaging template cuts through the clutter with a familiar sequence of statements that convey a journey or set of chronological events involving one or more characters who move through time and progress, or develop, during the process.

Each story, joke, parable, anecdote, or legend has innate power. Each has a beginning, middle, and end. That is to say, there is a "narrative arc" to the sequence of events that most people can follow.

Why does the story still work? Why is Hamlet performed or filmed anew each generation? Because the power of a compelling plot transcends time, language, and culture. Powerful fictional characters and a riveting plot command an audience every time. We are intrigued and curious and amazed all over again. Think of *Inherit the Wind, Dracula, West Side Story*, and *Les Misérables*. These tales will never leave the permanent tableau of mainstream theater.

THE TRANSCENDENT STORY

In fact, storytelling is one of the very few human traits or non-biological activities that transcend culture, geography, and history. Anthropologists find evidence of folktales and legends everywhere in ancient cultures, from Sanskrit to Latin to Greek to Chinese to Egyptian to Sumerian archives. The commonality of storytelling indicates something profound about human behavior and our evolutionary past. No doubt this is why we learn, process, and remember through stories better than through any other communication device.

Factoid: The oldest written story in human history is The Epic of Gilgamesh, written in Babylonia more than three thousand years ago. It describes a semi-legendary ruler of Uruk, an ancient city of Babylonia, near present-day Iraq and is often held up as the inspiration for the story of Noah. [Source: Learner.org]

Scientists are now beginning to agree that the universal appeal of powerful storytelling has a crucial link to social cognition—that is, how we learn about the society in which we live and how to navigate through this society.

Stories may act as "flight simulators" for life. A 2006 study at the University of Toronto indicated that students with more exposure to quality fiction tended to perform better on social ability and empathy tests. They were more familiar with ancient societal wisdom handed down in literature and legends, and they were aware of what the protagonists in ancient parables had learned by trial and error. In other words, such students were more perceptive, better communicators, and more likely to achieve better positions at work and to earn correspondingly higher salaries. By extension, this meant their children would have more amenities in life and better opportunities.

Welcome to natural selection in the modern era.

Another 2006 study, this one at Washington and Jefferson College in Washington, Pennsylvania, found relevant depictions of romantic love in folktales scattered across almost every prominent culture, even those with arranged marriages for economic or utilitarian purposes. Consequently, anthropologists now believe that romantic love must have roots in our common ancestry. The theory is that romance, not just sex, has a common biological basis in the brain.

Consider just a few basic cultural lessons and the classic stories in which they are conveyed:

- **Obedience:** Adam and Eve in the Garden of Eden from Genesis Chapter 3, *Curious George*

- **Work now, play later:** "The Ant and the Grasshopper" from *Aesop's Fables*

- **Stick to your character/be true to your values:** *The Odyssey, Star Wars*

- **Overcoming the odds:** *The Epic of Gilgamesh, The Legend of Sinbad, Mr. Smith Goes to Washington, Seabiscuit*

- **Man versus nature:** *Moby Dick, The Old Man and the Sea, Jaws, Twister*

- **Man versus monster:** *Beowulf, Dracula, The Blob, Alien*

- **Man versus the Devil:** *The Screwtape Letters, The Devil and Daniel Webster, The Devil's Advocate*

- **From humble beginnings to greatness:** *King Arthur and the Knights of the Round Table*, Joseph from Genesis Chapter 37, *David Copperfield*

- **Discipline and perseverance:** *Don Quixote, Oliver Twist, Robinson Crusoe*

- **Never too old to change:** *A Christmas Carol, Best Exotic Marigold Hotel*

- **Overcoming tyranny:** Moses from Genesis Chapter 6, *Watership Down, The Matrix, A Bug's Life.*

- **Believe in yourself:** *Aladdin, The Ugly Duckling,* the *Harry Potter* series

Throughout human history, as Joseph Campbell described in his seminal work *The Hero with a Thousand Faces,* three basic narrative patterns emerge in almost all cultures: romantic (Romeo and Juliet), sacrificial/redemptive (Noah's ark), and heroic (King Arthur and the Knights of the Round Table). Most popular, successful stories, regardless of era or the culture of origin, fall into one of these genres.

The point is that audiences accept ideas much more readily when their collective minds are in *story mode* rather than *analytic mode.* Attract more attention by appealing to the right brain instead of the left. Pastors, politicians, and clever marketers know this and exploit it, and you should, too.

For this reason, the vehicle to best communicate a Brand Echo is the story.

Take a look at some of the most effective newer marketing campaigns, all of which tell stories to advance a brand:

1. **In Gayle We Trust**, an original digital series produced by NBC/Universal and American Family Insurance. This quirky comedy about a hometown insurance agent and her oddball clients exemplifies public relations by sitcom.

2. **Thrive**, a series of branded YouTube videos by Whole Foods, explaining its food sources, vendors, recipes, and philosophy. Each mini-documentary tells an interesting short story about the people and/or products that make Whole Foods such a distinctive brand.

3. **TOMS Shoes CEO Blake Mycoskie**, who peddles philanthropy and footwear by giving away one pair of shoes for every pair sold in his online shoe business. Mycoskie often tells audiences "...the importance of having a story today is what separates companies. People don't just wear our shoes; they tell our story."

Here are some of the key principles when developing a message that can trigger a Brand Echo:

1. Identify a crucial NEED.

2. Solve the problem in a creative way, using EXTREME customer service.

3. Create an environment in which the customers EXPERIENCE your service.

4. Make that experience EASY to remember and re-tell.

FORMULATE AN ECHO

The last item above is crucial.

Be easy to remember and re-tell. Provide an EXPERIENCE that engages and enchants the customer.

What makes a story stick? What makes it powerful and memorable?

Chip and Dan Heath offer a recipe in their 2007 book Made to Stick.

Ideas that thrive, they suggest, are

(a) Unexpected,

(b) Concrete,

(c) Credible, and

(d) Emotional.

Not a bad mix.

Together, they can stimulate a powerful Brand Echo.

For example, Virgin Air claims it can "Make Flying Fun Again!" Does this concept resonate with people who are tired of the drudgery of modern air travel? You bet it does!

This claim is also unexpected. Flying isn't fun anymore, but most people want it to be. We expect drudgery and delays at airports. Fun is a remarkable surprise!

The claim is concrete, too. In-flight TVs for every passenger, mood lighting and WiFi on every plane. Food and drink are served on-demand, not in a 'one-size-and-time-fits-all' style. It's a treat.

Likewise, this claim is credible. If you've ever flown on Virgin you know they offer bright colors, light-hearted, even whimsical, airport signage, and a cartoon safety video to explain how the seat belts work.

Is the claim emotional? If you consider humor and delight to be emotions, then yes.

Consequently, every first-time Virgin Air passenger has an experience on the airline that is memorable and easy to convey as a story. "I arrived at the airport expecting one level of service, but experienced a WOW that was completely different!"

And who hasn't heard the story of the iconic CEO Richard Branson, who started selling used records on the streets of London and now owns several multi-national businesses? It's a great story!

Journalism, like almost everything in life, if done well, is both art and science.

The best in the business must know the basic ingredients, then blend them together with a masterful touch. They begin with an interesting focal point, or subject, facing a challenging problem. As I described in the last chapter, the issue or problem being addressed must have broad appeal. Then the journalist needs to know how to structure an interview, how to frame the narrative, how to avoid libel and slander, and other skills of the craft. (Makeup and hairspray are additional prerequisites for the narcissistic TV types, of course...)

The same can be said of law, painting, cooking, plumbing, golf, even surgery and psychiatry. Each relies on a body of basic knowledge, but the masters go well beyond the basics. Storytellers do the same.

The basic Brand Echonomics formula is simple: $(C + P + Y = Story) \times Ct = Brand Echo.$

That is, Client + Problem + Yoda (the expert with the great tool belt or light saber) = the Story. Multiply that by the Catalyst (Ct), or the delighted client who repeats the story, and you suddenly have a Brand Echo!

So, is the story about you? No. It's about the client. The customer. The guy with a problem to solve. You are Yoda. (Your company, product or service.) The expert. The problem-solver. Get it?

Recently, my wife and I went to dinner with another couple; they are long-time friends of ours. At some point, the conversation turned to financial matters, from saving for our kids' college tuitions, to mortgages, to life insurance, and so on. That's when our friends became very animated and spent the next five minutes telling us about the amazing service they'd received at a local bank, First Private Bank of Texas in Dallas. The institution has a relatively small footprint in the banking world, but an extraordinary commitment to customer service. The institution, we learned, not only refunds all their ATM fees but managers also helped simplify a complex real estate deal, curried cash to their home when necessary, and even offered to pick their kids up from school during a drawn-out meeting!

Our friends were amazed and impressed at the service. Dissatisfied with a large national bank, they'd been exploring personal banking options for several months. Having found a local bank with tailored and specific customer service, they were eager to spread the news. In so doing, they generated a Brand Echo. (And now I'm doing the same!)

In this case, our friends were the Clients (C). They had a distinct Problem (P) a lack of customer service at a major national bank.

The new, local bank and its account manager became the Yoda (Y). By offering an EXPERIENCE of superior customer service to address the Client's problem, a Story was born.

Our friends were the Catalysts (Ct) repeating the story, and now I too am a Catalyst, telling the Story of First Private Bank to a wide audience, which generates a Brand Echo—and it all started with great customer service, not a clever jingle or a billboard or even a new type of home mortgage.

That's the essence of a powerful Brand Echo. It works better than any other kind of advertising because it comes from trusted friends. I'm now very likely to consider becoming a customer at this bank, and so will other people, because our friends will no

> Stories make the issue (and solution) real, relevant, and memorable. We are hard-wired to remember stories. Stories follow the formula (C + P + Y = Story) x Ct = Brand Echo.

doubt repeat this story many times. What would happen to your bottom line if you had a brand ambassador or Catalyst who would do the same for your product or service?

Remember Carl Sewell, the successful car salesman?

In his book Customer for Life *he wrote, "Our job is to take care of the customer so well that he keeps coming back to us for the rest of his life."*

I would add to that, "And tells all his friends."

Now that you know the formula for telling a great story, what is the story you should be telling? Let's build it.

FOR DISCUSSION

What story is being told about your business today?

What story do you want to be told?

KEY #1: THE AUDIENCE

Understand the Client Better Than Your Competition

> The "C" in the Brand Echonomics formula stands for "Client." This person is the focal point of your Brand Echo. Lose sight of this and your entire business will suffer. The better you understand this person, the more successful your brand echo will be. Get to know him or her better than the competition does!

Next Secret:
Pay attention. Listen to the customer, learn and earn.

Too many of us are doing too little of this. A wise old reporter once told me to pay attention or I'd pay the price. It was sage advice, considering that libel and slander charges are always lurking in newsrooms.

As a recovering journalist, I want to share a personal story involving three very important questions that were asked of me at gunpoint. I now apply them to many aspects of my life, including business and the important work of building a Brand Echo. This is about the transformation of a vain TV celebrity into a real reporter.

It was January 1998. I was deep in a remote jungle somewhere between Chiapas, Mexico, and Guatemala. It was a misty morning—cool, quiet, and remote, even primitive.

I was a seasoned TV news anchor from the ABC affiliate newsroom in San Antonio, Texas. I was "the face" that delivered the evening news to a sprawling metropolitan market in South Texas. I was a celebrity—on billboards, writing autographs, and airing the big stories for an audience that stretched from Laredo on the Mexican border to Victoria on the Gulf Coast.

But now I was on assignment far from home, and it was a tense time in southern Mexico. I had traveled to the state of Chiapas, on the border with Guatemala, in the aftermath of a December massacre. Government authorities were in a long-term conflict with a leftist rebel army known as the Zapatistas (or EZLN). The rebel leaders had resorted to guerrilla warfare and terrorism as a means of forcing political change among government leaders they felt were indifferent and abusive. Mexico City had been put on notice.

Factoid: Chiapas is the southernmost of the thirty-one states of Mexico, bordered by Guatemala and the Pacific Ocean. Much of the state's history is centered on the subjugation of the indigenous population with occasional rebellions, the latest of which was the 1994 Zapatista Uprising, which succeeded in securing new human rights accords. [Source: Wikipedia]

To get the story, a photojournalist and I had traveled from San Antonio into the Lancondan Jungle near the Central American border to interview the rebel leaders. We were going to cover the political geoconflict by interviewing the mysterious rebel leader, and bringing home a series of news reports on the dangerous social and political climate in Mexico.

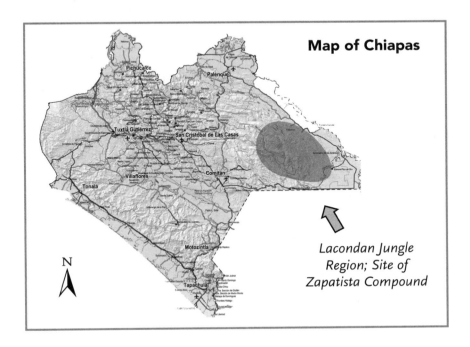

Map of Chiapas

N

Lacondan Jungle Region; Site of Zapatista Compound

The sprawling rebel compound, we soon discovered, was part jungle campsite, part fortress, and part refugee camp. The federal authorities in Mexico City had no governing control of this region, nor did the Chiapas state police or local law enforcement personnel. It was literally a no-man's land. The rebel leader, Subcommandante Marcos, was the one we needed to interview. He was nowhere in sight, but many armed militia members were on patrol, and to them we were intruders.

Suddenly, I found myself staring down the hot muzzle of an AK-47 carried by an angry Zapatista soldier. This had a sobering effect that few boardrooms or TV studios could match. I could see a bead of sweat trickling down the soldier's forehead. I could smell the carbon in the air. I could hear nothing but the sharp buzz of

Mexican cicadas high in the trees above.

This guy did not know or care about my celebrity status in the States. He did not want me to go any farther. He did not want to answer questions. Instead, he had three for me:

1. *Quién eres?* (Who are you?)

2. *A dónde vas?* (Where are you going?)

3. *Con quién viajas?* (With whom are you traveling?)

I'd spent my entire career asking pointed, pertinent questions and demanding answers. Now the tables had been dramatically turned. How I answered these three questions would determine if I got past the checkpoint, obtained the interview I needed, and came home with a powerful piece of media that would attract an audience. More importantly, two lives were on the line: mine and that of my news colleague.

In that moment, I was transformed from interrogator to the subject of the interrogation, from media star to humble servant. I was transfigured from a guy who wanted to explore and even exploit a foreign crisis for his own professional gain, to being a courier for a people who desperately wanted the world to know about their struggle.

I'd like to take each of those three questions individually and explain the connection between what I was asked in the jungle that morning and what you need to be asking your clients in order to develop a Brand Echo.

ECHO BUILDING QUESTION #1 – WHO ARE YOU?

After explaining that we had been allowed through previous military and civilian checkpoints because we were an American TV news crew on assignment, we were granted full access to the rebel compound. We interviewed the leaders. We shot video of a sprawling rebel camp with thousands of refugees who had been kicked off their land by government sympathizers. We even scooped the *New York Times*. The story attracted a big audience in South Texas and was a great success. Yes, I was fully aware that part of the EZLN strategy was to exploit media coverage—to amplify the impact of their rebellion. Still, they had declared war on the Mexican Government and many believed their cause had merit.

More importantly, however, through this experience, I gained a new and enduring perspective as a journalist and a human being. The most important piece of the communications process is understanding the audience. How well do you really know the customer you're trying to attract? Gaining the knowledge often requires tremendous effort. For us, it required travel, time, resources, and risk—lots of risk. In essence, we intentionally placed ourselves in harm's way to gain the trust of the Zapatistas and then we were able to tell a powerful story.

I'm not suggesting you go to the beach when a hurricane's headed ashore or that you visit a war zone, but I am suggesting that:

1. Developing a Brand Echo is hard work.

2. The process starts with gathering good information.

3. Asking the necessary questions that allow you to collect accurate and pertinent information may make you *feel* as though you're going into harm's way, but it's crucial.

Step #1 in Brand Echonomics: Aggregate as much relevant and current information as possible about the client. Accurate observations, survey results, and feedback provide the raw materials (data) of Brand Echonomics. They are critical to developing a Brand Echo.

Further, I would argue that if you aren't creating much of a buzz right now, it's because you probably do not understand your client very well. In other words, you haven't adequately answered the "Who are you?" question about your client.

WHAT DO YOUR CLIENTS REALLY WANT AND NEED?

Customer Relationship Management (or CRM), has always been important, but never more so than today. You have to understand your client and navigate the relationship. Period. Rule Number One for a young journalist is to *pay attention*, and the foundation of Brand Echonomics requires this same attention to detail. Asking the rhetorical "Who are you?" question about the customer is critical to developing a real understanding of the people you are attempting to attract and serve.

This sounds simple, but so few businesses do the research and ask the right questions. Instead, there's far too much guesswork and assumption at play. You *think* this is a great product or service. You *think* the customer will want it. You *think* you've addressed a real need in the market. But do you *know*? Why not find out? After all, the better you identify your client and understand her motivations and most urgent needs, the better you can deliver a product or service she'll buy.

Do the scientific work needed to discover the characteristics of your client and what her top priorities are. Is she a local, or did she recently move into the area? Is she a professional or a blue-collar type? Does she have a high school education or an MBA? Does she eat out at McDonalds or at the Ritz?

When I worked in TV news, we often tried to tailor our content for "Joe Six-Pack" or "Martha the Mom," whom we understood to be typical viewers. The right demographic profile in the right neighborhood. I had to ask myself what sort of news stories would appeal to those average citizens. We had to ask ourselves how to produce "news you can use" for the Joes and Marthas watching our program—how we could be more relevant to Joe and Martha.

Every merchant should do the same. He should always ask the following questions: How can I solve my client's most pressing need? How can I be more relevant?

Steven Covey wrote The Seven Habits of Highly Effective People *more than twenty years ago. Habit number five was "Seek first to understand, then be understood."*

Never was that advice more pertinent than it is today. Also, never has it been more ignored.

The companies that succeed in the modern economy will start by listening and understanding their clients best. If you want to be in this group, listen. Seek first to understand. Consider some of the following

- Regularly distribute a survey or electronic customer satisfaction questionnaire to your client. Read the results.

- Read client emails and listen to voicemails.

- Host what we call an OFFG, an old-fashioned focus group.

- Take a handful of clients to lunch and get some honest feedback.

- Ask the right questions that allow your customers to assess your job performance. If you can afford it, hire an agency to do the research and get some specific answers from a wide cross-section of your customer base.

Regardless of the tactics, get the low-down on your clients. And remember: "He who asks the best questions controls the conversation."

FLIP THE FOCUS

Carl Sewell believes in asking questions. His book *Customers for Life* details his formula for customer satisfaction. Chapter One, entitled "The Customer Will Tell You How to Provide Good Service," is all about eliciting feedback. At every Sewell dealership, every day, every time a customer sees a cashier, a simple survey is offered. Three questions are asked. They've evolved a little over time, but the questionnaire itself is always short and service-oriented: Did we repair the vehicle correctly on your last visit? Did we explain the charges? Would you recommend us?

Clear, concise, convenient. Carl Sewell wants to know.

It all gets back to understanding the client, and getting accurate data. How well do you know what drives that client of yours? Carl Sewell's three basic questions remind me of that simple interrogation in the jungle several years ago.

"Who are you?" This is the metaphorical question you need to be asking your client. Again the important questions are: Who is your average customer? Where does she live? How old is she? Is she married? Does she have kids? Where does she work? What does she value most? What story can your company tell to create a Brand Echo that matters to her? Better yet—what story would you like her to be telling?

The importance of this first step really can't be understated. Good information is the foundation of Brand Echonomics. Without a robust and accurate understanding of the customer, there can be no powerful brand message. No Echo. Remember that a brand is really nothing more than a promise. And a promise only makes a difference if it matters to the recipient. Recipients who are impressed by the promise and its delivery turn the promise into an Echo. That's the point.

This step is also the most frequently fumbled by brand managers large and small. Why? Because even if brand managers have good client information, they want to tell stories about themselves or their companies. They want to brag, gloat, puff, and promote. They want to describe their new product or promotion, their new store location, their new VP of IT, or their new regional director of business development, or some other drab topic. Don't do it.

I realize this truth may not be popular, but nobody really cares about *your* story until they have *their* problem solved. They care about *their* problem, so give me a story about *your* solution to *their* problem. That is, flip the focus of your brand story!

Simply put, Brand Echonomics does *not* involve press releases about new store hours or new hires. Brand Echonomics involves people telling great stories about how their problems were solved by your product or service. Period. You have to start creating an environment in which these great stories are inspired. This shifts the focus from *you* to building a message that matters to your *customers experiencing* an astounding level of service, then telling their OWN stories. Instead of a drive to achieve greater sales or store traffic, you want to provide meaning, and that's what really matters. That's what gets people talking.

Remember the three examples of provocative new brand-building strategies? None of them involve "what's for sale in the store" or "new hires" or even "new locations where you can buy our stuff." (Frankly, this is where most PR agencies fail.) Instead, they each involve something that happens with real people *outside* the store. Something beyond the reach of the retail operation, some compelling story that is of strong interest to the people who are likely to become patrons or clients.

Remember:

1. A humorous sitcom on NBC primetime. (The target audience needs something funny to watch on TV *and* needs auto insurance. Hmm...)

> Pay attention. How well do you know your best client? Pan for gold. What can you do to find out more? Flip the Focus. It's not about you; it's all about the customer.

2. A YouTube series about healthy food products, commercial fishing, and organic farmers. (The target audience wants more information about the food cycle and boutique, organic sources, and where to find them.)

3. A company giving away shoes in Argentina. (The target audience wants to help out low-income communities in a distant land...by shopping!)

So pay attention. Get to know your clients. Find out what compels them, worries them, or inspires them. Then do something about it.

FOR DISCUSSION

Who are your clients?

What story would introduce people to your brand and convince them you can do something important for them?

What sort of story would get people talking?

KEY #2: THE ISSUE?

Understand and Solve the Client's Big Problem. Be the Yoda!

The "P" in the Brand Echonomics formula represents the "Problem." This is the nagging itch which your competitors haven't overcome. It's the opportunity. The "Y" in the Brand Echonomics formula represents the "Yoda," or the wise counsel you offer. You are *not* the center of the story. You are the crucial resource by which the problem is solved. Consider this the "manufacturing process" of Brand Echonomics, or the system by which you've created a compelling new product or service. The "S" in the Brand Echonomics formula stands for "Story." This is your finished product in Brand Echonomics.

Secret stuff: Once you understand the client, you need to understand what key concern or problem she's trying to solve.

L et's go back to the jungle in Chiapas momentarily.

The smoking barrel of an AK-47 can capture your attention, particularly when it's pointed in your direction.

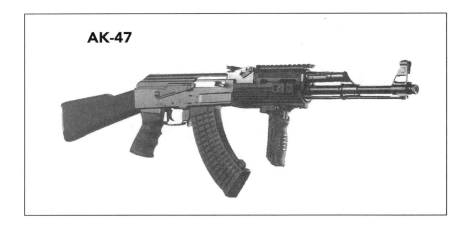

AK-47

The second key question I was asked at gunpoint in the jungle of Southern Mexico was, "Where are you going?"

The only thing the guerilla soldier wanted to know was my destination, but metaphorically, the question means much more.

ECHO BUILDING QUESTION #2—WHERE ARE YOU GOING?

That is, what is *your customer's destination*? What is her objective? What problem are you trying to solve for her?

Understanding the nature of the problem is critical to triggering the Brand Echo. And, of course, solving a problem requires understanding the problem. This is how the "Where are you going?" fits in. This second question cuts to the heart of the matter, which is this: What does your prospective client want or need? What could be keeping her up at night tapping away at Google? What problem is she trying to address?

Where is she traveling, metaphorically speaking, and what's the roadblock?

Step #2 in Brand Echonomics: "P" stands for "Problem." This is the critical flaw unearthed in the raw data. It could be inefficiency or lack of service a certain demographic is experiencing. What's the problem that your competitors have not been able to solve? Quality? Convenience? After-care? Figure it out and offer a solution. Your brand's real value in the Brand Echonomics formula is the Yoda. Your brand must be the problem-solver. It's the tool that comes to the aid of the customer with the problem. This solution is the real manufactured product of Brand Echonomics. This is the core of the message that drives the Echo.

Even if you know the client quite well, a brand message will fail if it doesn't accurately address one of her most pressing problems. Is she worried about spending too much money, white teeth, dropped cell phone calls, a safe car, termites, or air travel? Where can your brand step in and deliver the answer she's been seeking? Yoda introduced "The Force" to Luke Skywalker. It was a profound problem-solver. How can you do that?

Learn more about this client's top concern that aligns with the product or service you provide. Identify the itch, and then consider inspiring a story about how your brand scratches the itch.

So, the Echo is about your brand solution, but it's not about your brand. Get it?

In simplest story-telling terms, who's the bad guy? Stories aren't interesting without a problem to solve. When I tell my daughter a story at bedtime each night, she always wants a bad guy in the narrative. She's only five, but she already knows that stories are more compelling if there's a villain, a barrier, or a challenge of some sort. The bigger the problem, the more exciting the story. (If you're entertaining a five-year-old, you have to include a big bad wolf, a burglar or a bully.)

The more common the challenge, the more universal and more appealing the story. (If your target audience consists of twenty-five-year-olds, you need to know at least one challenge they are trying to overcome and address it.)

Then, your brand must become a Yoda, the eight-hundred-year-old Jedi master who represents the seat of knowledge in the Star Wars pantheon. That is, your brand should be positioned as the ultimate solution.

Next Big Secret: The key to developing a great Brand Echo is not a better storytelling technique or technology, it's simply a better story.

You must position your product, service, company, or non-profit as a better solution, then prove it, and the Brand Echo will originate automatically. Be worthy of the Catalyst and she will come. Be worthy of massive media coverage and it will come, as well. There's no shortcut, just a formula:

$$(C + P + Y = S) \times Ct = Brand\ Echo$$

This formula can be considered the manufacturing process of Brand Echonomics. How do you leverage the raw data (C) and the critical handicap (P) with your solution (Y) to create a story (S) that your clients will crave? That your Catalyst (Ct) will ignite?

SCRATCH THE ITCH

Consider Southwest Airlines. Over the last few years, the airline has made millions with the "Bags Fly Free" ad campaign, and it's easy to see why. If I'm the average American traveler in the middle of a recession, trying to get from one place to another on a thin dime, I don't want to have to pay for my luggage to travel with me. Everyone knows that bag transit should be included in the ticket price as it has been for decades. Southwest Airlines developed a powerful (and humorous) story about the problem, and then positioned itself as the Yoda with a great solution (with real SWA baggage handlers in the TV spots!). They nailed it with a multi-media campaign that reflected what every disgruntled airline passenger was thinking: *I shouldn't have to pay extra for my bags to travel with me!*

"We've clearly hit a passion point with the customers," said Dave Ridley, Senior VP of Marketing at Southwest.

According to Southwest, this campaign produced $2 billion in new revenue and grew market share by one full percentage point in just one year. Profits skyrocketed, and so did the airline's public perception.

In short, Southwest's "Bags Fly Free" concept created one of the best Brand Echoes in recent history. The campaign high-lighted a universal problem, solved it, and triggered an avalanche of stories in the process.

Other innovative businesses have solved other universal problems. If I'm the average American woman of an average American size who's grown up with decades of paper-thin actresses and models showcased in slick ads selling everything from lipstick to laundry detergent, I'm desperate to see someone like me in the media as an actress, ambassador, or spokeswoman.

The Dove Campaign for Real Beauty addressed the issue head-on using real women with real proportions as sexy, savvy models. This campaign touched a nerve among millions of female consumers who until then had felt isolated and ignored by corporate America. These women were elated to see other real women in the media. You can bet a Brand Echo ricocheted from coast to coast.

During March Madness in 2009, CBS and the NCAA knew that much of their audience would be stuck at work while the early games played, so they allowed games to be streamed online. Smart move, but what about the people with exposed screens or a chronic case of the-over-the-shoulder-boss?

Enter the "Boss Button." Tap it, and presto; watch your screen immediately switch to a bland, boring spreadsheet. Although the form was blank and the software didn't work too well for Mac users, it was perfect for PC-using basketball zealots working regular business hours. For them, the new "Boss Button" was indeed worthy of a Brand Echo. The network redesigned the software in 2010, and it has since become a staple of March college basketball.

Problems solved. Automatic Brand Echoes.

Or how about the new and improved laundry detergents, so concentrated you can get fifty loads out of one small bottle? Good-bye heavy, chunky, over-sized plastic jugs. Eureka. Another problem solved. Let the Echo begin.

How about the Square Card Reader, the plug-in device and application that makes any iPad or iPhone an instant credit card processing station? Oh, and it's free. Farmer's market vendors, cab drivers, even Salvation Army bell ringers say it's made life so much better. Brand Echo, anyone?

BRING ME THE FIX

Yoda the Jedi Knight had it right all along. In George Lucas' sprawling six-film space opera, Yoda taught Luke Skywalker to tap into an ancient, unbridled source of power. "May the force be with you." He understood something Luke had not been taught but could have tapped into all along, the knowledge that, "a Jedi's strength flows from the Force."

Yoda also had a relentless commitment to groom Luke into a Jedi knight, telling him, "Do or do not. There is no try."

This was great, counter-intuitive coaching, delivered in short, memorable snippets, and you know how it worked out for Luke Skywalker, right?

Years ago, I served in the U.S. Marine Corps. At a duty station in Arizona, our executive officer, Lt. Col. Clemmer, refused to allow me to bring him a problem without a corresponding solution. He would only listen to a complaint or a problem if I had a proposal for correcting it. He would say, "Bring me the *fix*, Lt. Brady! Bring me the *fix*!"

So—What is *your* fix? What is the powerful wisdom your brand can offer the consumer, and how can you make it easy for this individual to EXPERIENCE your fix, be delighted, and launch your Brand Echo?

PASS THE MEGAPHONE

The whole idea is to give your customers a script, a story, a jaw-dropping concept that is so spot-on relevant and valuable that they become instant ambassadors for your product or service. By touching a nerve, serving a cause, or solving a problem no other vendor has had the imagination or ingenuity to address, you make yourself both relevant and story-worthy.

To put it another way, the highly important data you collect is of zero value if you don't put it to use by solving a problem the client has identified for you. If you solve it effectively, affordably, and creatively, you *will* stimulate a Brand Echo.

No matter what you've paid the Manhattan-based Ad or PR agency, your messaging campaign, news coverage or slogan is not interesting to a potential new customer, to mainstream media, or to a blogger unless and until you find an incredibly innovative means of solving a common problem. Your message should somehow go beyond the industry average. It should inspire the crucial "Word of Mouth Marketing" or WOMM.

So, invest some time. Be of service. Remember Zig Ziglar's famous quote: "You can have anything in life you want, if you'll just help enough other people get what they want."

Remember the Rotarians: "He profits most who serves best."

Be the problem solver. No matter how well you understand the demographic makeup of your ideal client, if you misunderstand the key problem (i.e., the "road" your client is traveling), you will not be able to generate an effective Brand Echo.

Here's the key: The entire concept of Brand Echonomics is not about "spin" or a "gimmick" or a clever technology to get the right message in front of the right editor who will help sell your product or service on the right media outlet. In simplest terms, the best story wins. The premise is that your message has to earn the coverage by solving a prominent problem in a profound way. You must create a message that matters. The better the story you have to tell, the easier it is to generate a Brand Echo, and the farther it will travel.

> Know where your client is going and modify your business to be more interesting based on this data. Solve a problem. Do what no one else will do!

FOR DISCUSSION

Where is the client going?

That is, what problem is she trying to solve?

What is your Yoda solution?

Bring the Fix.

How can you position your brand to be Problem Solver and earn a Brand Echo?

KEY #3: THE CATALYST

Who Is Your Trusty Ambassador? How Can You Make it Easier for Her to Launch Your Brand Echo?

Word-of-mouth marketing trumps every other communications channel. It's more authentic, cost-efficient, and immediate. It's the distribution channel of Brand Echonomics. Simplify the concept to make it accessible, infectious, quick, clear, clever, and portable on any media channel.

Big Secret: We are a nation of tribes. Learn the language of the tribe you're trying to reach.

Seth Godin nailed it in his 2008 book, *Tribes*. We each belong to at least one modern tribe of culture and communication. Some of us are in several, based on our geography, education, profession, hobbies, or the media we absorb.

Even now, well into the automated, digital, data-centric twenty-first century, we are still a social culture driven by social needs. Most of us like to live in somewhat dense communities and to connect often with our preferred tribe, our club, or our den.

Technologies abound, but the single most powerful media platform known to mankind remains the human voice. The real engine that drives a Brand Echo is the personal advocate. We call this key component the Catalyst (Ct), the catalytic converter, the distribution channel of Brand Echonomics. This is the person who has the influence and the reach to realistically introduce and convert many new clients to your brand, and it calls to mind that third powerful question that must be asked: With whom are you traveling?

In 2000, Malcolm Gladwell referred to this cadre of influencers as "connectors, mavens and salesmen" in his bestseller The Tipping Point. *These are the chatty, well connected few who are most likely to pay attention to brand messages, aggregate the information, and steer others toward particular concepts.*

According to anthropologists, about 1.8 million years ago on the plains of Northern Africa, one Homo Erectus used a crude language to tell a story to a friend from the next cave. It may have been about a great place to pick grapes, catch fish, or meet the ladies. Regardless, it was the birth of word-of-mouth marketing.

Back then, the only communication tool available was the voice. It was simple, common, convenient, and universal, and it was sufficient for many thousands of years.

We've come a long way since that modest beginning to the Golden Era of Mass Media, circa 1999, when one voice from a newsroom in Manhattan or an Oval Office in Washington,

DC could reach more than a hundred million people at once. Remember the eve of the Millennium? I was anchoring the news in San Antonio that night when so many suspected a computer meltdown would stop the world on its axis. It never happened, of course. But we imagined it would, and counted down the seconds as one global media village.

Factoid: Archeologists believe the Phoenicians developed the first written alphabet in about 12,000 B.C. By about 4000 BC, the Egyptians created what we now call hieroglyphics—mostly for cave wall artistry. A short time later, the Chinese started writing things down on bones. [Source: ENotes.com]

Love it or lament it, those halcyon days are nearly over. Mass media still commands a giant audience, but only occasionally. Aggregating one audience on one media outlet at one time for routine content is quickly becoming a rarity. The massive, all-powerful footprint of mass media is now in decline. Most big metropolitan daily newspapers are in bankruptcy or in distress mode compared to the reach and profit margin they enjoyed only a decade ago. Most TV audiences are smaller, too.

SHRINK THE AUDIENCE

What media platforms are on the rise? It might surprise you, but the so-called "niche" publications and specialized cable and TV programs are exploding in popularity. Not all of them, of course, but the best voices with the best content are attracting impressive audiences, as are the polished podcasts that only appeal to a motivated community of zealots or enthusiasts in a narrow interest group. Search iTunes University for podcasts on literature and you'll find detailed MP3s from the New York Public Library, Prairie View A&M or the University of Glasgow on esoteric topics like Shelley's *Frankenstein* and the letters of Bess of Hardwick (she was the second richest woman in Elizabethan Britain). Now those are narrow audiences, but in a digital landscape, it makes sense for iTunes to offer them. *(This "deep catalogue" of digital content was described in* The Long Tail *by Chris Anderson, Editor of* Wired *magazine.)* The same goes for blogs, as well as e-newsletters for artisan cheese-makers or coin collectors or homeschoolers or alumni of particular colleges. What we often call "mini-media" platforms are ascending to prominence. No single niche content provider can command the kind of goliath audience that the giant TV networks once attracted, but together they do.

In this new era, brand stewards need to recruit more than foot soldiers and occasional advocates. They need Catalysts to tell the stories, even if the platform (or reach of that advocate) is small. One powerful Catalyst can be the tipping point of a sweeping Brand Echo. Find the niche 'content provider' who is speaking to your ideal demographic, and that will be the channel to reach your Catalyst.

My favorite channel to communicate or grow a brand is still the journalist (see Chapter 10)—and generally speaking, the most visible type of news remains the TV broadcast. However, it has changed and so I must offer this warning:

NEWS AS A COMMODITY

Today, the technology of mass-media distribution as a whole is alive and well, but the varied channels and outlets have become so numerous that they are virtually invisible. The irony is that they are simultaneously everywhere and nowhere. This is especially true for TV news. Penetration may be high, but the influence of traditional mass media is at an all-time low. Few viewers really pay attention to daily TV news these days. It has become an electronic commodity that's available, but largely ignored and irrelevant. It's really more like wallpaper than a precious resource. There are many reasons for this, including:

- The proliferation of technology,

- The abundance of news outlets and sources, and, in many cases—

- The philosophical distance between the news source and recipient. An isolated, detached, and pampered news anchor in a cool, automated studio in Manhattan, LA, or Dallas seems disconnected from the reality of everyday life in a small town in Texas, Idaho, Illinois, or Pennsylvania. I know because, for many years, I was that detached, smug anchor in the chilly studio.

Worse, it's a one-way monologue. The news anchor "pronounces" the news to viewers from his lofty perspective instead of engaging us with impactful information about what affects our lives today.

Newspapers can be even more isolated and irrelevant. Consequently, most big metro newspapers are on the verge of bankruptcy. Most cable and network news organizations are fighting for a fraction of the audience share that single TV organizations once controlled. On the other hand, online video providers and many small community newspapers are thriving.

The massive old communication models are less and less pertinent in a society that expects media to be immediate, mobile, and specific. In the not-too-distant future, what I call the "nichecast" will overtake the broadcast as the preferred delivery platform for news and information.

Right now, for instance, TV newsrooms in my hometown of Dallas, the fifth-largest media market in the country, are tasked with tracking down the most riveting events of the day in an enormous swath of North Texas that includes parts of more than twenty counties populated with nearly seven million TV viewers. Is a deadly wreck on a highway in one county of interest to viewers in all twenty counties? Nope. How about a pronouncement from one school superintendent, one robbery at a mall, or one flooded river? Not really.

What would be of tremendous value, however, would be a town-cast or even a neighborhood-cast devoted exclusively to my immediate neighbors and local schools and businesses. We have the technology to do this, but we lack the business model to make it economically feasible. Nonetheless, I predict it will happen soon. Newsrooms of the future will be convergent mash-ups that aggregate professionals and amateurs, broadcast and digital, with kids and seniors delivering content pertinent to their demographics and neighborhoods.

In the interim, the most relevant media I receive is from my inner circle: the people who know my family, my employer, my friends, and my neighbors. If they believe a political candidate is worthy, I'm likely to be influenced and possibly vote in a similar fashion. If they recommend a laundry detergent, I'm likely to buy it. If they provide a positive review of a new movie, I'm likely to see it myself. Why? Because they know me and my interests. They walk the same sidewalks and shop in the same grocery stores.

A new survey from the Pew Research Center and Knight Foundation reveals that fifty-five percent of adults say they get local information weekly or more often via word of mouth from family, friends, co-workers, and neighbors. Respondents also indicate that news or information has greater impact because of the trust and proximity of the source. Most of us who know the industry suspect this figure may actually be much higher than fifty-five percent.

Accessibility, believability, and local relevance are tremendously high within our "inner circles," but the further out the media source, the less impact it has on my immediate world. See the Media Intimacy Index below for a look at the relevancy of various forms of media today.

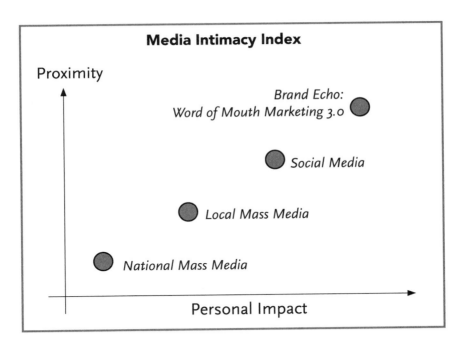

As described in Chapter One, the single most important message to be delivered about your product, service, company, or cause will *not* be delivered by you or even by some agency or advocate you hire. Instead, it will be that authentic and casual but compelling endorsement of your brand made privately by one friend to another. This is the Brand Echo reverberating from one satisfied customer or Catalyst to a new consumer. The more intimate the source, the more powerful the recommendation. The more frequent the recommendation, the greater the impact.

BETTER SOLUTIONS CONVERT

The minds behind the Social Media Collective, or SMC (my term for the cabal of the four most popular social media sites of Facebook, YouTube, LinkedIn, and Twitter), and the most prominent search engines are all well aware of the Media Intimacy Index. Witness the mad dash to provide local relevance to your search. We're already seeing it with Google Plus "hangouts" and "circles" as well as Facebook nuances that include more intimate angles of our personal lives.

In light of all this, how can a brand solicit ambassadors with a message, or Brand Echo that ripples across the connected digital media universe to help "influence the people with the greatest influence?" What is the 'Yoda' you can offer to address the client's greatest need? How can you entice the Catalyst to tell your story?

First, remember our formula: (C + P + Yoda = Story)

Second, offer a better solution. Remember, the more important, widespread or painful the problem you can solve, the more powerful your Brand Echo.

Third, make it counterintuitive if at all possible. Make it unusual. Do what no one else is doing. The more unique your

solution, the better your story. And the more memorable. Remember the Heath Brothers' recipe included the unexpected and concrete.

Fourth, keep it simple and short! No one has time to read a dissertation.

Quick + Clear + Clever + Counterintuitive = A Better Story.

As mentioned before, a clever commercial can be enough to broaden brand awareness and trigger some interest, but in the modern media landscape, a standard ad rarely elicits sales unless it involves a great and true story. Offering the client an immediate solution and a unique approach, coupled with an unrelenting commitment to superior service, almost always triggers a powerful Brand Echo. Try it!

Look at how hard BP worked to get real people telling real stories about the oil giant's cleanup and restoration efforts along the Gulf Coast after the disastrous 2010 Deepwater Horizon explosion. Was it effective? Depends on whom you ask, but the campaign was carefully produced to be authentic, powerful, and in some cases, counterintuitive. BP and its executives were not at the center of each short story. Instead, real people told real stories about real solutions. The damage was too great for this campaign to trigger a powerful Brand Echo, but each little story helped stem the horrific tide of bad media surrounding BP.

A completely DIFFERENT example of a powerful, serendipitous story that triggered an Echo was "The Miracle on the Hudson" involving the January 15, 2009 U.S. Airways Flight 1549 piloted by Captain Chesley "Sully" Sullenberger.. After a flock of geese unexpectedly flew into the plane at takeoff and disabled both engines, Sullenberger landed the plane on the Hudson River with no fatalities. Did the airline trot out executives to talk about airline safety? No way. Sullenberger and his crew were the media darlings, telling their story to dozens, if not hundreds, of media outlets in the following weeks. "Yes, we saved the day by landing our plane on the Hudson River. Yes, we did what no one has ever done before, what no one anticipates, what no flight crew would want. But we saved everyone onboard!"

The approach was quick, clear, counterintuitive and clever. It launched an enormous Brand Echo for U.S. Airways.

I know it's pushing the metaphor to its limit, but come back with me one more time to Chiapas:

The third key question I was asked while staring into the barrel of an AK-47 in the jungle of Southern Mexico was "Whom do you have with you?"

The last thing the guerilla soldier wanted to know was the identity of my colleague. Who was travelling with me—to help get the job done?

Who was my ally?

The same questions applies here, as well

ECHO BUILDING QUESTION #3 — WHOM DO YOU HAVE WITH YOU?

Remember, the most powerful concepts, the most effective messages, and the most believable stories about your brand will be those concepts, messages, and stories you *do not tell!* Your

Catalysts will deliver them for you, virally and automatically.

Again, these are the people who have encountered your brand, have been delighted with the service or the "fix" you have offered, and who then share that experience with others.

> The best distribution model of Brand Echonomics is to recruit ambassadors by solving problems. Delight your clients, and you will be helping them write a script to spread your Brand Echo.

Step #3 in Brand Echonomics: "Ct" stands for "Catalyst." This is the crucial engine that drives the Echo, the ambassador who recruits other ambassadors. Find out how to provide the exemplary experience for her, and on what media platform she most often communicates. (Next chapter!)

This principle cannot be emphasized enough. Even Coca-Cola, Apple and Kimberly Clark do not have an ad budget big enough to deliver the brand message as far and wide as each CMO would like it to travel. So even they—each of these giant brands—must rely on Catalysts to get the Brand-Building job done. Particularly in this era of BIO-Media. (Remember?) Success requires that Personal Stamp of Approval.

The most effective tool to reach and influence your next client will be the person that client knows and trusts, the person with whom that client is "traveling." Equip your ideal Catalyst to tell a great story about your brand. You won't know exactly who this individual may be, but by setting the stage for a specific type of experience, time after time, and exceeding the expectations of your most loyal clients, you will enable the Brand Echo.

FOR DISCUSSION

Where are your potential Catalysts?

What platforms constitute "BIO-Media" for her?

How can you Shrink the Audience to reach her?

How can you make it easy for your Catalysts to start your Brand Echo?

LANGUAGE LESSONS: FINDING THE RIGHT CHANNELS

Waste Not, Want Not.
Avoid Becoming Media Clutter.

> Most media is wasted because there is no compelling message; the channel does not match the intended audience, and the recipients are not engaged. Avoid the waste!

Counterintuitive Big Secret:
You can start the Brand Echo by spending less.

To trigger the Echo, you want a powerful impact on a committed, captive Catalyst who will become your evangelist, rather than a forgettable impact on millions.

You also want to be as cost-efficient as possible. Again, this is another application of accurate data.

Have I mentioned it enough? The best media campaigns rely on powerful stories that will be experienced, owned, and transmitted by word of mouth, which is still by far the best medium through which to pass along information. Or, as David Meerman Scott says, by "word of mouse." We are now living in an age when micro often trumps mass-media. Today, the popular blogger with a powerful following can be just as effective in reaching the right audience as network TV.

Remember the scene toward the end of "Finding Nemo" when all the animals in the sea pass along the riveting story of the clownfish father who fought his way across the Pacific Ocean, all the way to Sydney, Australia, to find his long-lost son Nemo?

That's the essence of a powerful Brand Echo. The Personal Stamp of Approval. Everyone who hears it takes ownership and passes it along. It's driven by the relevance, value and emotional impact of an amazing story that touches a nerve. Every parent and every child can identify, on some level, with the idea of facing any challenge, going any distance, and overcoming every obstacle that postpones or inhibits this reunion. So the question now becomes: What solution, what act of service, what effort on *your* part could generate a "Nemo Factor" that would spread organically across your city or industry?

And please remember that we all occupy different media real estate. Just because you read it or watch it or listen to it doesn't mean everyone else does. As I referenced in Chapter Seven, we live in a nation of media "tribes," more so now than ever. If I grew up watching my dad read a particular newspaper every morning over a cup of black coffee, I may be predisposed to do the same, but the guy in the next booth at Starbucks is very likely reading something else on his tablet. Very likely.

Today we live in a digital "land of plenty," and that means content of any shape and size is available 24/365. The only way to sort through the full-throttle fire hose blast of information spraying across our dashboards every day is to systematize the process by using some regular gatekeepers. We all do it. We frequent those media "stations" that best service our needs, professional or personal:

I like the political slant of this network, so I'll make it my default TV station for news...

I enjoy keeping up with my friends across the country, so I check Facebook first thing every morning...

My email is still at Yahoo, so I scan the headlines on the Yahoo homepage every morning at work...

I can't give up my morning newspaper...

Some still consider the *Wall Street Journal* the gold standard of American news coverage. If the *Journal* doesn't cover it, members of that tribe don't see it, and it probably doesn't have much consequence in their professional world.

If another tribe uses Yahoo mail, then the Yahoo homepage may be the filter of choice, simply out of convenience.

Some use Mark Zuckerberg's social network as the go-to portal of "news" required for frequent news updates during the day. Others prefer one of the old-school standards, ABC, NBC, or CBS, as long as they can accommodate—or TiVo—the old-school news-media "feeding times."

Yet other tribes listen to talk radio, ESPN, or NPR. Maybe they read online resources like the Huffington Post or the Daily Beast.

The point is, be objective and judicious. Understand that the media YOU seek out may not be what your client seeks out. And you can't afford to be everywhere. Make smart decisions about the media your ideal client consumes and find the ideal 'watering hole' for the Catalyst you are trying to reach. A great deal of cash is wasted in advertising today because of all the bad decisions made about where and how clients consume news and information.

I believe there are four primary "wheels in motion" across the modern media universe, and you'd better have a hand on all four if you want to be effective. These four platforms: organic, social, earned, and paid, are simply the channels by which your Catalyst can deliver the Brand Echo.

To learn more, read on.

8

ORGANIC MEDIA: GROW IT YOURSELF

Don't Wait for Matt Lauer!

> Tell the story yourself. Hire a freelance journalist to write, record, design, videotape, and/or edit the piece. Get it *exactly* right. Show it off.

Big Secret: the era of "push" media is fading; "pull" media is on the rise. That is, attract an audience, don't assault one!

We are in the midst of a dramatic and foundational shift in the way our culture accesses, digests, and interprets media content. Have you noticed?

Historians will look back one day and see a tremendous digital and generational divide developing during this time period. Those of us who typically fall into the "Boomer" generation tend to recognize and rely upon traditional forms of mass media and to discount new platforms like LinkedIn and The Daily Beast as unproven and unreliable.

Younger generations trend in the opposite direction. They are attracted to new digital sites and disregard conventional print and TV newscasts such as NBC Nightly News and the *New York Times* as dull and dated. Find a college student and ask if he or she subscribes to a newspaper. Fat chance.

Ultimately, each media platform can be tremendously effective in reaching a broad audience. Yes, millions of people still watch The Today Show to be fed a daily digest of top news and information. But many millions more surf YouTube daily, seeking specific content pertinent to their immediate interests, hobbies, or profession. We occupy a highly blended media culture. And while word of mouth may be the name of the game, some tangible and easily accessible website usually is the star of that game. Or at the very least, a starting point.

Facebook may be the chatter at the coffee shop, but it's only a tool. It has become such a Wall Street leviathan that almost every new iteration and storyline gets coverage in mainstream media. And—with its own team of publicists and media agencies in tow—it has a ponderous web footprint. American Idol still reaches people initially on network TV, but the highlight migrates quickly to YouTube. Media channels today are inextricably linked.

Factoid: Ninety-six hours of video are uploaded to YouTube every minute. (Although I'm fairly certain that number will be eclipsed by the time this book is in print!) [Source: YouTube.com]

My experience has been that the right message tends to reach its audience. Even a short, simple press release, if well composed with an effective central message and distributed digitally, can get extraordinary attention.

In the midst of this modern landscape, it amazes me that so many intelligent, competent business owners, entrepreneurs, and even marketers still believe that the only way to reach a broad audience is to "wait on NBC" or another brand of the somewhat dysfunctional mass media machine to tell their story. These CEOs and CMOs, usually Boomers, often pay extraordinary sums to PR firms or other "influence" agencies to ramp up campaigns that will attract the attention and elicit the coverage of professional journalists. And yes it works—sometimes. Half the time, it does not. (And I'm being generous here!)

Even the most stable, serene newsrooms are chaotic today. Journalists are swamped. More assignments, shorter deadlines, and fewer colleagues with whom to share the workload. They don't have time to listen to your dull pitch. And no, Matt Lauer will NOT be returning your call, much less coming for the interview!

Here's the good news:

The attention, coverage, and distribution of traditional media helps, but its only one channel by which to reach your ideal audience.

In today's convoluted and crowded media environment, you are very often defined by what you publish, produce, and circulate. So instead of relying on NBC, why not:

- Write a blog about the little-known but best practices in your industry

- Create an info-graphic about the dramatic changes in your industry, then post it online

- Produce a white paper about the most dangerous trend in your industry, post it on your website, then distribute a press release about it

- Produce a podcast series on the top five things every consumer should know about your industry

- Shoot a video series about the biggest misconceptions about your industry

- Interview an industry icon and write a short Q&A with him or her, as a downloadable PDF for your homepage

While this is the golden era of content marketing, I prefer the term "organic media" because the very best content is usually homegrown, authentic, direct, natural, and not overly produced. The more sophisticated the audience, the less likely it is to be impressed with a slick commercial. Instead, the value of the content is directly related to the problem being addressed. If it's funny, all the better.

Author and speaker David Meerman Scott in his 2007 book The New Rules of Marketing & PR *said it best: "Great content brands an organization as a trusted resource and calls people to action to buy, subscribe, apply, or donate."*

Further, he says that, "Organizations gain credibility and loyalty with buyers through content, and smart marketers now think and act like publishers in order to create and deliver content targeted directly at their audience."

He's right.

Think about it. You could easily spend more than twenty or thirty thousand dollars on a professionally-produced television commercial. It's not too dissimilar from a short film project: the location, the talent, the lighting and sound, the writing, the shooting, the post-production editing...Then you have to buy the commercial time to put the finished product on the air. It gets extraordinarily expensive very quickly, and the only people who will see it are those who happen to be watching the right channel at the right time. Of that audience, how many are potential buyers?

My point: There's a lot of waste in traditional advertising and PR.

Compare those strategies with a sample YouTube video that you could shoot, edit, and upload free of charge. Video cameras are cheap to rent or buy, and your potential audience is global! And it's free. Even if you hire a professional crew to create the media, it can populate your website or YouTube channel and reach a potential global audience in perpetuity—for a remarkably low cost. Obvious perhaps, but often neglected.

FROM PUSH TO PULL

We are moving from the "push" marketing era of advertising, much like a carnival barker who shouts to command the attention of an audience—to the "pull" marketing environment of an artisan baker who creates delicious aromas that naturally attract interested buyers passing by.

To put it another way, for the last one hundred years, a one-way media channel that pushed media at the audience according to a rigid schedule has dominated our society. Now a media landscape is evolving in which producers and contributors from anywhere can create content and post it anytime for anyone to see. And the audience can respond. Often instantly. And the best content— positioned in the best context—usually wins.

Push v. Pull

Push Media	Pull Media
Uninvited	Invited
Unrelated	Related; Pertinent
Uni-directional (One-way monologue)	Interactive
Scheduled	On-demand
Expensive	Inexpensive
Old	New
TV Commercial	YouTube

Put this knowledge to work for your business by using organic media/content marketing to tell the audience firsthand what you're doing and show your snazzy new product or service to the world. Demonstrate your expertise, establish yourself as a leader, and then let the market decide the real value.

Yes, it's intimidating. Gutsy. Even risky. You might be thinking, "What if they don't like me?" "Do I have to be funny?" or "What if my content goes nowhere online?"

Might happen. But if so, what have you lost? Not nearly as much as if you'd used a similar concept and bought a lot of TV or radio time.

Besides, it's very doable. Media technologies are more advanced and more affordable than ever, the barriers to entry are lower than ever, and your work is more visible than ever. We take it for granted today that we live in a global village in which we can record a video on a hand-held device in Dallas, upload it, and be visible immediately to people in Del Rio, Damascus, and Dusseldorf, with no TV, satellite signal, or cable required. The same is true with an e-book, article, photo, or audio clip. All media, all the time, is available all around the world. If it's optimized properly, it works wonders for your website visibility. Just find the right keywords (Google will provide these) and make sure that any media you add to your site is appropriately tagged with the same terms.

Suddenly, you're optimized. You're visible. You're the online expert. Just make sure all this new stuff has a home base on your website. Then you can farm it out on appropriate collateral sites after that.

The internet is jam-packed with stories of people who uploaded content and quickly became internet sensations. Even better, it's packed with small businesses that grew big with viral videos and other content. Check out:

- **Will It Blend?** by Blendtec, an enormously popular video series on YouTube

- **The T-Shirt War**, another wildly popular video by Rush T-Shirts on YouTube

- **Thrive**, a web-video series by Whole Foods

- *Knock Knock* by Seth Godin, his first e-book before he became the mega "new media" celebrity

- *Implementing Six Sigma*, one of the most downloaded white papers

- **The Adam Corolla Show**, which holds the Guinness World Record for the most downloaded podcast

- **Kony 2012 Campaign**, a short documentary by Invisible

Children, Inc. that has profiled a Ugandan guerilla leader, with the intent of launching a global campaign to have him arrested

The point is, none of these products or concepts were launched with mainstream media or major mass media outlets, yet they've each reached millions.

Don't be afraid to do it yourself, or to recruit freelancers to help get it done internally.

Don't wait for Matt Lauer. He isn't coming.

DO IT YOURSELF MEDIA

The bottom line is, you know your topic, product and service better than anyone else. And hopefully, by now, you know your ideal customer better than ever, so why not talk to her directly? If you've done your research properly, you know what problem she's trying to solve. You can address that need immediately and specifically, with no filter or intermediary.

Keep in mind that the media you produce and publish to populate the "hub" of your brand should drive everything else. That doesn't mean your company has to hire a full-time copywriter or videographer to churn out gobs of content just to fill up endless web pages, but it does mean you should find some way to start producing at least some appropriate and well-developed content that is pertinent to your industry and your clients.

There's a reason Harley Davidson and Whole Foods and Patagonia don't do as much traditional advertising as their competitors: They understand the power of organic media. They understand the barriers of BIO-Media, the appeal of "DIY" messaging and the new rules. Learn a lesson from these successful campaigns and reach your new customers directly with media you produce and own.

Remember the "Questions from Chiapas" that you need to answer about your clients before you can create a compelling story that will impact them:

1. Who is the client? (the "C" in the Brand Echonomics formula).

2. What is the Number One problem your client is trying to solve? (the "P" in the Brand Echonomics formula). How can you answer her most pressing needs? (the "Yoda" in the Brand Echonomics formula).

3. And lastly, how can you create an experience to delight the Catalysts?

Deliver your answer in a short article, audio podcast, or unique video (my personal favorite), and you will be on your way. And remember, this content feeds everything else—social media and potential news coverage as well.

It will position your company as a thought-leader in the space. It will demonstrate your ability to solve problems with authenticity and approachability.

Now, I understand the pushback. You don't have time to do this, correct? You don't have time to eat lunch, much less buy the camera and editing software, learn how to shoot and edit, then come up with several great ideas each month as subject matter, plus hire someone to produce the video series.

Got it.

So hire that freelance journalist, copywriter, podcast engineer, or video crew. There are a lot of us out there who want freelance work. You might put an ad on Craigslist, or call one of your local TV newsrooms and ask to speak to the chief photographer.

Ask for anyone doing freelance video shooting. You might also ask for the best two or three freelance photographers in the area. (Believe me, you will want to pay a little extra for someone who knows exactly what they're doing.) Make sure you see a demo reel before hiring anyone. After all, any photographer worth his salt has an amazing "show and tell" file on a jump-drive today. You can also call the metro assignments desk of your local newspaper and ask for the contact information of some talented freelance writers. They will respond. Believe me, everyone needs the extra cash these days.

> Don't think you have to wait for the professional journalists to find you and tell your story. This is terribly wrong! You can get nearly as much visibility with content you produce yourself.

The point is, get your story out there, even if you have to hire someone to help you tell it.

FOR DISCUSSION

What organic content does your website have?

What organic content does your website need?

How could you get it produced?

CHAPTER

9

SOCIAL MEDIA: START A CONVERSATION

It's Not Your Story Anymore!

> Social media is not an option anymore. It's a necessity for business. Branding is a dialogue. Engaging the audience means listening and responding, and that happens primarily on social media. First, find the right platform. Then listen. Then engage. Do not sell. Contribute good advice and observations. Chat. Be social. Serve *first*!

Another top-shelf secret: Social media is social. Consider it a party. Be present. Be authentic (don't outsource). Contribute. Serve others. Don't brag. Be gracious.

I can't spend much time or effort on the "tools and tactics" of social media because they evolve daily. If anyone claims to be a talented and effective "Social Media Expert," beware. No one is an expert. We are all students and primarily self-taught practitioners. The landscape changes that quickly.

109

So, what are the strategic basics?

Be polite. Listen. Watch. Learn. Be yourself. Be honest. Be transparent. Don't fake it. Lighten up. No showboating! Give credit when and where it's due. Help others. Don't expect much. Come back over and over. Invite your friends.

These are what I call the "Sandbox Rules" of building your Brand Echo using social media. Any tactical concepts beyond these basic tenets, most of which we all learned in the sandbox or on the Wii playground years ago, are outdated as soon as they are written. Believe me, there are people trolling the internet right now, jacked up on caffeine, writing the code for the latest Facebook iteration or designing a new version of Pinterest.

Digital technology evolves by the second. New social media channels, sites, and software systems arrive daily from developers and entrepreneurs around the globe. More and more of the innovators are in Bangladesh or Beijing, not Austin or San Francisco. Regardless, the changes are relentless. As a business owner, manager, franchisee, or entrepreneur, you can certainly get lost in the weeds on this. The updates never end. Keeping current can be a full-time gig. The questions are constant:

How do I create a video for YouTube? Do I need to be funny?

What kind of camera do I buy? Where can I find the best deal? How much should I expect to pay? What features do I need?

Where can I learn to edit? What editing software do I need to buy?

How do I post a video so that it is "optimized" for web visibility?

How do I engage with prospective clients on Facebook?

How often should I be Tweeting, and what's the best way to include links and URLs?

The questions go on and on, but here's the bottom line: You can go to your local big-box bookstore and find many tomes on the "best practices" of social media, but the four most important concepts remain constant.

HONOR THE MOST IMPORTANT PRINCIPLES

The first of these critical concepts is to plant the flag. Having a social media platform is crucial, unless your business only targets a very small, older demographic or a very geographically isolated audience. And ONE POST is not enough! Be timely and consistent. What? You mean you've heard this already? Look, using social media is cheaper, faster, and, if used properly, more believable than any other media, but we still don't have a good, reliable way to measure the infamous ROI (Return on Investment) or ROE (Return on Engagement).

We will have a tool to create these metrics soon, but that day isn't here yet, so lower your expectations.

I know, I know. This drives the MBAs and other metric-oriented folks among us crazy. What? Investing time and resources in a function or marketing campaign that doesn't generate tangible results? Well, yes.

Second, on the flip side, it's still important to set goals. What are you trying to accomplish with the big social media dialogue, anyway? Analyze the social media universe and decide where your brand needs to have a presence. Keep it simple. Maybe just raising awareness is enough. If you're already on multiple platforms and you've lost control, pull back. Shut down one or two conversations, if necessary, in order to improve your efforts on the most important platform. More fans and followers sound great, but why? What do you want to communicate to that audience? Keep in mind, if you treat them like a captive TV audience and start shoving obnoxious advertising at them, they will evaporate.

Factoid: The consulting group Gartner recently found that seventy-four percent of consumers rely on some sort of social media to help them make buying decisions. Still, another recent survey showed that most companies do not have a comprehensive Social Media plan. "One of the keys is to know what you're trying to accomplish," says Scott Nelson, a Gartner analyst who focuses on social media strategies for enterprises. "Doing social media because everyone else is doing it is not a strategy." [Source: Network World]

Third, as fellow Texan Dr. Phil says, "Get real." Be transparent. Be authentic. Be yourself. Social media communities can smell a veiled sales pitch ten miles out, and anyone offering one will quickly be ostracized.

Also beware: If you outsource the entire conversation to someone who's never even set foot in your business, you are undermining the basic premise of social media. Having an indifferent third party tweet or post or blog for you is akin to being invited to the White House, the Super Bowl, or an Oscar party and sending an intern from someone else's company. It makes no sense. The whole idea of social media is to foster honest, genuine conversations between real people. If you outsource the conversation to an outsider, you're basically handing off that brand extension to someone who doesn't really know your brand.

Of course, I understand that many companies are earning millions of dollars handling social media campaigns for clients today. It's a profitable business model that employs plenty of so-called "digital natives" and puts plenty of executives at ease. "Whew!" goes the thinking. "We've effectively addressed the 'social media' issue by hiring Super Social LLC to run our Facebook campaign." If your only purpose is to 'robo-tweet' or generate daily posts, then go ahead—hire an agency, sit back, and relax. Mission accomplished.

But if, as I would suggest, your bigger purpose is to start conversations with people who want to know more about your brand, you are going to find yourself in trouble. Think about it. Your entire campaign will end up in the hands of a junior account manager (Tiffany or Tanya) who knows nothing about your business. When a real prospect responds to something that junior account manager has tweeted, how will Tiffany respond?

Here's the key—if you must outsource, make sure the agency or social media coach knows your brand intimately, and is equipped to speak for the company.

Lastly, help steer the conversation. Don't smother it. Get comfortable with the fact that the entire brand identity and the companion conversation are not yours alone anymore. You *share* the concept with avid fans (or at least you hope they're avid).

The best conversationalists consistently add value to the encounter. Offer tips, suggestions, best practices, ideas, contacts, examples, analogies, jokes, or better yet—stories—that pertain to the topic or situation. What was your experience? What did you learn? Who is a great resource? Is there an event scheduled soon that might be helpful? Even better, offer a resource of your own: a book, article, or recent blog post. Contribute a URL to a (short) recent cover story or a news item—especially if it's one in which you are quoted! Just be certain that the material is pertinent to the topic at hand, clear and concise. No one wants a lecture or a textbook—even if it comes in 140-character blasts.

And one more thing—get tough! Grow a thick skin. Understand that not everyone will be a fan of yours, and that's okay.

HERE TO STAY

I like to make the comparison between social media in the early twenty-first century and the telephone in the early twentieth century. Social media is truly nothing more than a tool for communication. Sure, it sounds bizarre at first to the oldest among us. A common response is, "Why chatter with a bunch of so-called 'friends' you never see? Seems like a huge waste of time! I'd rather be running a business! I don't have time to waste on Facebook, in a chat room, or reading blogs!"

But if we had a time capsule and could travel back in time about one hundred twenty years and observe post-Civil War American culture, I imagine we would hear businesses and homeowners making dismissive observations about a new invention that was just beginning to creep into public and private areas. This newfangled device of Mr. Bell's connected people's voices over long distances and allowed them to carry on conversations even if they were in different buildings or cities or states!

The business owner of the late nineteenth century probably said something like, "What a waste! I don't have time for any silly electronic children's game. That telephone is a waste of my employees' time and effort!"

Of course this is ridiculous. Today we clearly understand how extraordinarily powerful a tool the telephone is.

Factoid: Contrary to common opinion, many inventors helped develop the technology behind the first telephone. Although Alexander Graham Bell received the first commercial patent, Innocenzo Manzetti, Charles Bourseul, Johann Philipp Reis, and Antonio Meucci preceded him scientifically. [Source: PBS.org]

Social media is equally powerful. Like the telephone, it's a critical communications tool. Indeed, the younger the audience, the more likely they are to be on Facebook or Twitter. Several photographers I've worked with in the past have given up email entirely and only correspond by text messages and Facebook. One of my clients is the president of a commercial roofing company based here in Dallas and is a LinkedIn fanatic.

Social media is here to stay, but we are in the embryonic stages of its development, and it changes extraordinarily quickly. Pinterest is the newest craze, but that too will evolve. By the time you read this, another extraordinary site will have emerged.

FOUR LAST REMINDERS

The key to developing a Brand Echo on social media involves four basic principles as opposed to tactics related to one specific site.

First, No Selling! Social media is socially based, not transaction based, so don't try to sell. Think of it as a party at which you want to be social and considerate. Listen first. Contribute, but don't spend much time promoting yourself. It's tacky at a cocktail party *and* on a social media site. Contribute ideas. Refer a friend. Suggest a TV show or an editorial you recently enjoyed.

Second, Keep It Close. Assign an internal CSO, short for Chief Story-Telling Officer, who will be in charge of the entire social media footprint for your company. This should be someone within the company who knows the brand and is competent speaking for the CEO.

In other words, as I said before, **do not outsource your entire social media campaign!** This is the unspoken cardinal sin on every social media site. If you need to hire a coach or consultant to help, do it. But handing over the keys to your entire social media footprint is treacherous. If you do this, sooner or later you will be "outed" and likely discredited. The basic premise of social media is to generate authentic, transparent, and value-forward content in a dialogue format. If you farm out your social media to someone in a cubicle who knows nothing about your brand, you've immediately sold out.

Better to give the job to someone who knows the company and sits right outside the boss's office. Be transparent. The Brand Echo conversation has to be *real*!

Third, ROE not ROI. That is, Return on Engagement. The best strategy for developing a Brand Echo with social media is to focus on engagement rather than immediate profit. Sounds simple, but the bean counters in your management team will demand some accountability from the external social media rep who began the engagement. Remember, it's better to have a solid (but small) core audience than an army of people who don't care.

Fourth and finally, Keep Current. Engage your viewers/ listeners/readers by posting new content on a regular basis. Tell a story weekly to keep them coming back. Better yet, figure out how to create such an atmosphere of service that your brand ambassadors, your Catalysts, start telling stories for you. Put up a sign or two in your retail space, in your office, or even online as a reminder.

Just try to not use the often-abused reminder to "Follow us on Facebook!" Not many people want to be followers. Instead, try "Join our conversation on Facebook" to let your customers know where to find an important online community with relevant information. Just a suggestion. Not every commercial environment is the same.

> Be transparent and casual, yet work to build authentic, personal relationships and to establish your executive team or your company blogger as a thought leader in your industry. Recognize that the brand message is largely in someone else's hands. What consumers say will be heard and believed *far* more than what you, the company owner, ever say.

FOR DISCUSSION

Who is your CSO? (Internal or External)

What are your social media goals?

10

EARNED MEDIA: ATTRACT THE BIG BOYS

*News Coverage Still Matters.
(Just Not As Much.)*

> Journalists are still the best, most reliable gatekeepers for accurate, accessible media. Traditional mass media platforms still matter. Pitch a journalist the smart way: be media-worthy with a solid Brand Echo first. Tell the story on your website. Establish a footprint in social media. *Then* solicit news coverage. Do your homework, practice the pitch, be persistent, have more than one idea, and seek to serve first.

L et me be frank.

Journalists are hard to impress. They are frequently overworked, underpaid, and stressed over the migrating business model. Their world is changing rapidly. They are often indifferent, callous, tired, blunt, or even caustic. (Been there, done it. Not proud.)

On the other side of the proverbial coin, journalists can be highly engaging, curious, inquisitive, articulate, determined, exuberant, and even flattering if you have a compelling story that fits within their beat.

The Common Thread: Journalists—whatever their mood du jour—will gravitate toward a powerful story.

So recognize a trend here.

Next Big Secret: The compelling story sells itself. Journalists want to cover TOPICS, not produce commercials for your product or service!

When was the last time a reporter asked your opinion? What was the occasion? What was your response? Was the resulting story related to your business or your industry? What sort of visibility and affirmation did that opportunity render? Has a journalist ever sought you out as an expert in your field?

News coverage works. It becomes a stamp of authority and a badge of honor because you:

(a) Borrow the brand visibility and credibility of the news organization,

(b) Obtain the posture/position of industry expert, thought leader, or authority within your industry, and

(c) Reap the benefits of widespread distribution.

One caveat: It's an affirmation and a plus, but it's honestly not as big a deal as it once was. Getting a story on the ABC World News broadcast means about eight or nine million people will see it. That's a big audience, but only about three percent of Americans overall. A similar percentage applies to most local TV newscasts.

It's an important piece of the pie, but only a piece.

That said, news media still gets seen, read, and listened to by a broad audience. Many pundits have been quick to promote the "death" of mass media or the slow demise of traditional journalism, but folks, it ain't happenin'. Fewer "monster" TV outlets dominate a single city, fewer big metro newspapers exist, and fewer powerhouse radio superstations command the attention of millions. But those hard-core news products developed today are more likely now than ever to get traction and be picked up by numerous other news organizations, or aggregators. Going viral isn't far-fetched. We recently had a story shot and edited by a news crew in Dallas that aired at an affiliate station in Norfolk, Virginia, before it even aired in Dallas!

The best-case scenario for your Brand Echo is that one of your advocates is so amazed with your product or service that he or she mentions your brand to the media. If that doesn't happen right away, you can pick up the phone yourself.

But first, let me help you make that pitch to the media by "pulling back the veil" in modern newsrooms so that you can start off correctly, something very few people—or PR agencies— manage to do.

EIGHT SIMPLE STEPS TO SUCCESS IN PITCHING TO A JOURNALIST

Before I get to Step One, let's make sure you aren't wasting anyone's time. Are you pitching something the journalist is likely to cover? Better yet, are you pitching a topic she's already covered? Sometimes that's a great hook: "I have an idea for a new story related to something you covered six months ago. It might be a great follow-up!" You see, I'm a recovering journalist and I know this crowd well.

First, the state of the news industry today:

For the most part, newsroom salaries have come down and workloads have gone up in recent years. What industry hasn't suffered a similar plight in the Great Recession? The fact remains that most journalists, whether print, broadcast, digital, or "new" media, are doing more work for less compensation and less recognition. Both their ranks and their wallets are thinner, and they no longer have the once-vaulted distinction of working for the prestigious Fourth Estate. Nobody really knows what that means anymore, and no one really cares.

Journalists today also know their audience is scattered, that traditional media consumption habits have eroded, that the overall media landscape is something akin to the Wild, Wild West, in that few rules remain, and that the rules that do exist evolve daily.

But one thing remains constant: Well-produced original content—in the right context—*is still king*, and working journalists still produce most of it. Not Tweeters, YouTubers, or bloggers. In fact, the social media mavens usually rely on journalists to provide source material. All the Google coding and algorithms from Boston to Beijing won't mean squat if someone doesn't produce original content to be collected, crunched, and categorized.

To earn the attention and affirmation of the press, a few proven strategies remain that work every time, even in the modern media rodeo.

STEP ONE: DEVELOP A GREAT BRAND ECHO

You may be tired of hearing this, but tired or not, you need a succinct and distinct narrative with a beginning, a middle, and a powerful ending. You need a protagonist, a barrier, a Yoda who has a clever and unusual solution, and you also need a successful conclusion. In other words, you need a great Brand Story.

Some local examples from the greater Dallas area speak volumes:

Problem: A local shopper finds a good price on a new Trek bicycle or a pair of Nike shoes, but are these the best prices? He wants to know before making the purchase.

Solution: ShopSavvy, a Dallas-based technology firm, offers a mobile app that will scan a product's bar code and immediately report on the best local price for that product. This was a great story, and it received a lot of publicity. People were talking.

Problem: Dallas has a huge church-going population, including one of the country's largest lesbian, gay, bisexual, and transgender (LGBT) crowds. Where can gay and lesbian Christians worship?

Solution: Cathedral of Hope, the world's largest LGBT Christian church, celebrated its fortieth anniversary in 2010. Pretty cool story, regardless of your theology.

Problem: All pizza looks, feels, and tastes the same. Dallas' burgeoning foodie crowd is demanding something better.

Solution: Dough, a start-up pizza restaurant ships a two-ton wood-burning stove made of volcanic rock directly from Naples, Italy. The idea is to produce authentic Naples-style pizza using the volcanic stone-heating element. A great video shows the stove being delivered by crane. Super idea. What TV station wouldn't want the "volcano oven" on the 10 p.m. news?

Remember, great stories sell themselves. The harder you have to work to get the journalist's attention, the less appealing your story.

STEP TWO: MAKE SURE YOUR WEBSITE REFLECTS YOUR PITCH

Why is this important? It's very simple: Your website will be the first place a journalist goes to verify your story. It should be the "hub" of your Brand Echo. It all starts here.

Journalists are lazy, like the rest of us. As soon as they hear an interesting pitch, they'll try to verify it. If your website doesn't mention the concept being discussed, or at least allude to it, and offer credible, current contact information, the viability of the pitch is eroded, so make certain your idea is front and center in your website.

Make it easy to find, simple to understand, and downloadable. Media press kits are the best. If you don't have one, consider it.

STEP THREE: DO THE RESEARCH TO FIND THE RIGHT REPORTER

Once you have a great story, find the journalists who cover this industry or topic. Start with Google and search for the specific topic in Google news. Find the reporters who posted the stories. If you have access to a journalist's database like Vocus or Cision, even better.

Gather a list of at least ten viable journalists along with their phone numbers and email addresses. You might start with trade journals, but their newsrooms usually consist of about two people. They will often be more likely to accept articles and columns written by guest contributors.

For instance, if you want to pitch a story about high-end pet grooming, you might need to find someone who writes about luxury brand experiences, upscale lifestyles, or upscale retail. It's really not hard to do. Thirty seconds and one Google search later, your list will start to grow. Now you have a few names. Then it's back to Google to find email addresses or newsroom phone numbers for those journalists.

STEP FOUR: DEVELOP A RELATIONSHIP WITH THE JOURNALIST NOW

This is vital. Reach out as someone who cares about media coverage in your industry and journalism and "getting the story right." Do this *before* you have a story. Make contact. Establish the relationship. Seek to serve first. Ask the journalist what sort of stories he likes to cover and tell him you'll be on the lookout. If you develop the relationship now, with no specific agenda, you've initiated great newsroom access *before* you have something to pitch. Believe me, it works much better this way. Better, because news coverage should be continual, like a long friendship, not a one-night affair.

Start by pitching a story or two that have nothing to do with your company, product, or service. Demonstrate your knowledge of the industry. Ask the reporter how he likes to be contacted and what sort of third-party verification he needs before a story is printed, published, or produced. You'll gain a lot of respect. *Then* suggest a story involving your Brand Echo.

STEP FIVE: ORGANIZE THE STORY WITH ALL THE REQUISITE PARTS BEFORE YOU CALL

If you're lucky enough to get a live reporter on the first call, you want to be ready. Your pitch will be much stronger if you've already identified the protagonist at the center of the story who had a problem and how he or she solved the problem with the use of your product, company, or service. Find a customer or client who will talk to the media.

Remember, the story's not about you, but about the "C" with the "P."

Do as much of the heavy lifting as you can. Assemble all the parts: Issue, Expert, and the Person with the Problem (does this sound a little familiar? C + P + Y) so that you make it easy for the reporter to pick up the story.

STEP SIX: BE DIRECT, SPECIFIC, AND PERSISTENT

Call the journalist you've identified as being your best contact, but don't be a stalker. Yes, it's a thin line to walk. Ninety-nine percent of the time, you'll be talking to voice mail. Leave a tantalizing message, a "tease" so to speak, short and seductive.

Here's the best phone message to leave: "Hi, Bill. This is Jeff Brady. I enjoyed your article on bicycles and biking. Thanks for the coverage. I have a great story idea for you that affects hundreds of people in our city. No one else has written about it yet, and I think you ought to be the first! It's highly controversial, but I have several people who will talk about it. Here's my phone number… Thanks!"

STEP SEVEN: BE HONEST

Never lie. If you do, you'll eventually be caught. When you're caught, you're finished. Sounds obvious, but sometimes the obvious items deserve to be mentioned up front.

STEP EIGHT: HAVE MORE THAN ONE STORY READY TO GO

If the reporter shoots down your first story idea because it sounds too much like something he covered six months ago, you'd better have a plan "B." Otherwise, he may know you're just pitching a single client.

Here's the bottom line: Seek first to serve. Instead of calling the journalist up to get him or her to do what *you* want, why not contact several reporters in your newsroom of choice to find out what you can do to help them? Be of service. Ask what sort of stories they want to cover. Maybe you can help find some great, undiscovered gems. Offer your service first, as a loyal reader, listener, or viewer. Help the reporter do what they do. Then you've laid the groundwork to describe the work you do, or your cool product or service.

Once again, a great story sells itself. If you have an innovative, creative, distinctive, proven solution to an issue or concern that touches a lot of people, you will get the attention you seek. It's similar to the formula I outlined to make the story appealing to

> Journalists are jaded, hard to impress, and overworked, but they still provide most of the original news content. Impress the press with authenticity and specialized knowledge, and then offer your observations.

your brand Catalyst: ensure the pitch is quick, clever, clear, and counterintuitive, and you'll have most of the hard work done!

FOR DISCUSSION

Who are the top five journalists in your home community who cover your industry?

How can you contact them?

Begin a relationship by asking what sorts of stories they really want to cover, and offering yourself as a resource.

PAID MEDIA: THE LAST RESORT

Awareness, Yes. Believability?
Not So Much.

> Commercial advertising remains a multi-billion-dollar industry, but its shrinking effectiveness is undeniable. Consumers are jaded, skeptical, and indifferent to most ads. Overcome the barriers by focusing on the Catalysts who can spread your story. Does your message get traction on YouTube?

Next Big Secret: Advertising is losing it effectiveness, yet still it survives. Use it for awareness only. Find a way to TARGET all ads. Generic campaigns are wasteful.

The multi-billion-dollar ad industry has more agencies, accounts, and activity than ever before. Yes, some traditional agencies are staggering and conventional ideas are on the ropes. But advertising is here to stay.

That said, advertising is generally considered to be the most expensive and wasteful means of brand message delivery. It's also the most temporal, the most unidirectional, and the least credible. Whether a billboard, radio, full-page magazine spread, or a glitzy TV commercial, the public today typically turns the other cheek to whatever conveys your ad.

While massive ad campaigns still promote massive brands, these messages aren't quite as dominant as they once were because the three previous platforms—organic, social, and earned media—consume more of the traditional media budget.

So while the eulogies may proclaim that advertising is obsolete or even dead—it survives. Modern ad campaigns, however, often take a subsidiary role to PR, and the evolution is underway to a smarter, more diverse, and more mobile industry.

Ads are getting both more dramatic and, in some cases, more discrete. They are migrating to newer, heretofore sacrosanct, spaces (school buses and high school football stadiums, for example). They are evolving into clever product placement campaigns, and they often get a trial run on YouTube or a blog before launching on primetime TV, billboards, or a Facebook fan page.

Case in point: Both the Google and Facebook empires have been built with billions of dollars spent on what's increasingly known as "smart" advertising. In other words, the ad only plays when a potential customer has already entered the buying cycle and has voluntarily begun searching for a topic related to the item advertised.

This means the traditional ad model, not to mention the traditional ad agency, is in trouble. In just a few years, both may be extinct. But advertising will still be here, as will advertising companies and coaches. They will just look dramatically different.

BACK TO THE FORMULA

Ads still work, but not as well. They should only be a part of the overall brand-delivery campaign, not the majority. The key is to target the campaign. How can you reach the specific people who are already likely to buy—and considering your brand? The Brand Echonomics formula still and always will apply. Start by finding the Catalyst. If the message works with this individual, it will appeal in an advertising campaign.

Remember the conversation about media barriers and BIO-Media? We TiVo, we unsubscribe, we block, and we delete. The new barriers keep unwanted media out of our lives, but smart media and smart ad campaigns get invited in.

Consider the recent Super Bowl commercial starring the boy dressed as Darth Vader who tried to get his family's household appliances to respond to "the Force." In the end, he attempted to animate his dad's Volkswagen Passat, and Dad helped with a remote starter. Voilá! The boy was amazed by his powers and everyone in the world was entertained.

That commercial immediately went viral because it was extraordinarily creative and entertaining. It told a short, clever story. Boy had a problem. The technology of Volkswagen solved the problem, with Dad's help. Charming.

This cute narrative sequence was *not* focused on a "buy" message. The story wasn't even centered on Volkswagen; it was centered on the boy. Viewers identified with the boy and wanted to see him succeed. He had a problem (okay, not a big one, but an objective, nonetheless) that the product could solve.

$C + P + Y = Story$. Short, clever, endearing narrative. Once everybody started talking about it, the rest of the formula kicked

in. The Catalysts did their thing; the story took off, and ta-da!—
Brand Echo. Genius.

Old Spice, Apple, and Chrysler have also produced compelling
commercials and released them on YouTube alongside network
TV, and the results have been dramatic. Like the Super Bowl
commercial, these ads have spread organically.

Offer something terribly useful or an enormously entertaining
story (or both), and you will recruit advocates who build your
Brand Echo automatically, enthusiastically, honestly, and free of
charge.

*Factoid: While targeted advertising can be extremely effective,
London-based Fournaise Marketing Group recently announced that
global ad effectiveness sank twenty-one percent in 2011. Specifically:*

- *B2B ad campaigns were particularly impacted: their effectiveness
  fell by twenty-two percent, while B2C campaigns fell by nineteen
  percent.*

- *Even online ads have seen a downward spiral and were sixteen
  percent less effective compared to the same period a year prior.
  Online display ads took the biggest hit, a thirty-eight percent
  decline and third-party database email campaigns were next,
  with a twenty-nine percent decline. Ouch. [Source: Fournaise
  Global Marketing Effectiveness Report]*

Still want to pay for that ad inventory next year? Let the buyer
beware!

Here's the take-away: Consumers, buyers, customers, and
clients don't pay as much attention to ads as they did five years ago.
If it's an unsolicited, generic message, it will be largely ignored.
Consumers are increasingly tuning out the advertisements and

relying on word of mouth. The more intimate the source, the more they pay attention. (Remember the Intimacy Index?) The more apparent that the source of the media message is a cabal of "creatives" in Manhattan, the less relevant it is.

So, would it be possible to create an oral, grass roots, and brand-building campaign without advertising? Yes.

THE BEST STORY WINS

Here's the key: The best stories reverberate. They create Brand Echoes. And they either supersede the need for paid advertising or they set the stage for a highly targeted advertising campaign that is both cost effective and memorable.

Let's consider a few hypothetical concepts:

Example: What if a prominent airline decides to let all active-duty military service members fly free of charge anytime they are home on leave during the Christmas holidays? This might be announced in a corporate blog entry, then in a U.S. Army press release, then in news stories during the holidays, then in a huge Twitter campaign about helping heroes get home where they belong. Talk about a Brand Echo with a huge ripple effect! No ads required.

Example: Consider a nationwide food company announcing that it will no longer use beef and poultry producers who do not follow animal husbandry practices approved by the Humane Farming Association. This could be announced in a press conference, then in a video series on YouTube, then the local media pick it up in Texas and Idaho, then a few national papers and a network pick up the story, then a massive grassroots movement highlighting "respecting the food chain" and healthy living. Yep. That would do it. No advertising necessary.

Example: What if the Breeders' Cup needed to re-energize horseracing season, so it finds a celebrity horse that can dance, guzzle Guinness, and win races in amazing, come-from-behind finishes? A series of videos is produced, then the horse has her own Facebook fan page, then she makes a series of appearances on morning TV, then a press conference is carried live around the country, and finally a big ad campaign promotes the horse at the Breeders' Cup. OK, this one is real. Kudos to the Conover Tuttle Pace marketing agency in Boston for creating this great Brand Echo for Zenyatta! An ad campaign was only required toward the end of the media cycle, when many other channels had been exhausted.

Example: What if a major fast food label wanted to attract attention to its college scholarship program. How to go beyond the usual high school essay? One well-known brand used the Weber Shandwick PR firm to launch a Twitter contest highlighting the scholarship with the best tweet winning the cash. After it was announced in *USA Today*, the scholarship tweet campaign generated more than a thousand media placements and tens of millions of media impressions, including two AP stories, multiple stories on CNN, MSNBC, The Weather Channel, and NBC. Not bad.

The program also captivated the online world, generating more than nine million social media impressions as a result of tweets during the brief entry period. In all, more than 2,800 applicants tweeted for their chance at $20,000. The KFC Twitter handle saw a twenty percent jump in followers in just two weeks.

One of those followers was seventeen-year-old Amanda Russell, whose tweet, "Hey Colonel! Your scholarship's the secret ingredient missing from my recipe for success! Got the grades, drive, just need cash!" scored her the $20,000 college scholarship.

You see? It works! The best marketers, media mavens, and storytellers already know this. The best story wins because it's the easiest story to remember and repeat. That's the key. So think of yourself as a scriptwriter for your own product or service. What will

> Non-targeted advertising is usually a tremendous waste. Can you ensure most of the people who see your ad will be potential clients? Facebook and Google have built empires on the practice!

people actually remember about your product or service? What's the best possible endorsement? Now write the script. (C + P + Y = Story!)

Just remember: Imprecise advertising is a dangerous, wasteful business. Even if you have encouraging data about the audience, you are taking a huge risk that your audience will happen to be watching, listening, or reading when your story is served up. Even if a large audience can be reached with the primary distribution, how many of those are likely to become clients, not to mention repeat clients?

Focus on telling a great story and keep the paid advertising as a last resort.

FOR DISCUSSION

How can you extend your Brand Echo with a very small, highly targeted ad campaign?

(Hint: LinkedIn works well. So does YouTube.)

BIGGER THAN BUSINESS

The Epitaph You're Writing Today

> Life trumps business. The eternal brands matter. If you were to attend your own funeral, what Echo would you hear?

Biggest Secret: A Brand Echo is about more than making money. It's about meaning, relevance, and EARNING attention, not buying it. Create a message with your life that matters.

Ministers, rabbis, shamans, and imams know about powerful Brand Echoes. They understand concepts that have a ripple, or a shadow, or an eternal footprint. It's a natural familiarity because, culturally, they are the people we lean on most often to remind us of the most deep-seated eternal brands—those we ponder at the most crucial times in life: baptisms, marriages, and funerals, where science drops off and sheer wonder begins.

For example, we can calculate and commoditize the financial burden of marriage, the high degree of risk, and the improbability of success, but those numbers drop away when the right person arrives. There is usually a ceremony to recognize the union, and a spiritual leader is called upon to summon powerful brand messages.

We can analyze and scrutinize the biology of human reproduction or the extraordinary modern cost of raising a child, but the science and finance all fades to insignificance when that beautiful baby arrives. And there is often a ceremony to celebrate and welcome the new child into the community in which the spiritual leader is expected to summon the eternal brands. Get it?

Likewise with death. We can ignore it for a lifetime, and most of us do. We can concentrate on growing a business, earning a higher income, and acquiring a bigger house and vacation home, but when death beckons, all those matters pale in comparison to the life we lived and the people we loved most. The people we married. The babies who arrived, then grew up in a flash, and then had babies of their own.

Eulogies are all about Brand Echoes.

So yes, the concept of a Brand Echo applies to more than business relationships. A Brand Echo transcends commercial marketing. Like it or not, your family has a Brand Echo. Good or bad, helpful or hurtful, it's there. Your neighborhood has a Brand Echo. So do your Alma Mater, your company, and your work.

And yes, *you* have a Brand Echo, too. What do people say after you leave the cocktail party or the softball field, office, synagogue, or banquet?

Do you lift spirits or depress them? Do you encourage your friends and colleagues, or discourage them? Do you add value to your relationships, or bleed them dry?

Your personal Brand Echo is about a lot more than profit and loss statements and cash flow. It's even about more than the promises you keep. It's about the ripple you initiate in the lives of others.

The Brand Echo concept, applied individually, is actually about the personal footprint of your life. How do your kids talk about your behavior to their friends? How does your spouse describe you to her sisters? What will be written in your epitaph or spoken in your eulogy? Whether we realize it or not, each of us is developing a Brand Echo that will follow us in life and after. It's not about being obsessed with public opinion or popularity; it's about having an impact and serving the community in which you live.

YOUR LIFE'S WORK

I have a friend who's a marvelous pastor in the Dallas area. He's been at it long enough to have plenty of weddings and funerals under his belt. At death, he tells me, the survivors want to hear three things only: (1) that the deceased is reunited with the Creator/Source, (2) that it's healthy and human to grieve, and (3) that the good work enacted by the deceased will be remembered.

We all want to know that the ripple, the powerful Echo of a life well lived, will reverberate long after the memorial service or the funeral.

Simply put, a life's work is bigger than transactions. It's about creating some type of positive change over a large period of time for people who are connected to one another by blood, workplace, church, club, community, or friendship.

Few in our Western culture like to talk about it, but sooner or later, the end comes. So what happens then? Regardless of your concept of an afterlife, what ripple will you leave behind? That ripple, whether for good or bad, is the most significant and permanent Brand Echo of all.

MAXIMIZE YOUR CHI

What's a PBE and Why Does it Matter?

A Personal Brand Echo (PBE) is that brand message that surrounds a person in life and after and is often summoned in a eulogy. Your life force, or Chi, is the seed of your Personal Brand Echo (PBE). Journalists typically have the opportunity to encounter and learn from many people. So do you. Pay attention. The PBE can transform your life and the lives of many others.

Chi (pronounced 'chee') is frequently translated as life energy, life-force, or energy flow. Chi is the central underlying principle in traditional Chinese medicine and martial arts. The literal translation of "Chi" is breath, air, or gas. [Source: Wikipedia]

Next to Last Secret: Personal Brand Echoes mean more and last longer than commercial Brand Echoes.

W e remember people over products. Monumental architects like Frank Lloyd Wright more than the buildings they designed; captivating actors like John Wayne and Elizabeth Taylor more than the movies they brought to life; gifted athletes like Don Meredith, Junior Seau, and Wilt Chamberlain over the teams on which they played; and visionary business leaders like Walt and Roy Disney, Al Davis, or Steve Jobs over the companies they created. We honor the legacies of great individuals who drove, inspired, or served great concepts, works of art, athletics, business, education, or design. These are the individuals who push our culture forward.

Some higher calling—some life force or inner drive—some Chi—almost always drives these people. Building a powerful and productive PBE almost always requires tapping a higher power. In *The Shift*, Wayne Dyer says "we must become more like the spiritual nature of our origin." Agreed. Actualized individuals—people like the ones I occasionally had the pleasure to meet and interview—have done it.

What is your higher power? What is your Chi life energy, or life force? Where do you become centered? In Sanskrit, the term is *prana*, meaning "vital life." In Japanese, it is often called *reiki*. In the Hindu culture, the term *chakra* is often used to represent a life energy. In Western culture, most Christians refer to a similar but not identical concept as the "Holy Spirit." And, of course, George Lucas introduced audiences to a somewhat similar Hollywood metaphor when he gave Obi Wan Kenobi the line "May the Force be with you."

No, I'm not an evangelist or even an educated philosopher, just an observant journalist. During my career, I have seen a remarkable kinship between people of varied backgrounds who share this inner spark. I believe it would be negligent of me to outline the entire Brand Echo concept and not make the profound observation that it applies to far more than market share.

Corporate Brand Echoes are retold in the marketplace, in corporate boardrooms, and at Stanford, Wharton, Kellogg, and SMU. The Personal Brand Echo is retold at the dinner table and at the graveside. Which matters more? Most would say the latter.

THE JOURNALIST'S PERSPECTIVE

Most reporters, by virtue of the job, have opportunities to meet and interview remarkable people from all walks of life. Time and time again in my role as a reporter and anchor, I found myself interviewing newsworthy people who had achieved some accomplishment, milestone or award—due largely to a strong life force that drove them further than anyone else. Some inner calling, drive, passion, or vision ignited the action that led to the accomplishment. They usually pursued some 'big picture' agenda that others ignored, and believed they were aligned with a cause that was bigger than them.

I also found these people to be the happiest and most fulfilled people because they were committed to doing something productive and they wanted to share a skill or ability with the world. They wanted to give back, to educate, serve, inspire, build, create, or improve their immediate surroundings with the tools they had at hand. They were contented people who were at some level in touch with their Chi, Holy Spirit, or life force. It's not baloney; it's real.

Some I interviewed were street sweepers and garbage collectors. Others were surgeons, senators, or symphony musicians. The profession rarely correlated to the personal commitment to service. Doing the thing that they knew best to improve *that* street corner, patient's heart, concert, in *that* moment was all that truly mattered.

Each was serving the immediate community in a way that produced a profound Personal Brand Echo. Individuals were immersed in a process or profession that so completely tapped their inner being, their Chi, that it was completely fulfilling. The person gave of himself or herself entirely. The promises made were fulfilled immediately, and any expectations were usually surpassed.

Psychologists and behavioral therapists often call this "being in the zone" or "flow," as coined by a 1960s Hungarian psychology professor named Mihaly Csikszentmihalyi. It means doing something you enjoy completely, at which you are talented, and by which you serve a larger neighborhood or community. The means by which you solve problems.

But this concept is about more than problems and promises. It's about energy and delight. It's about finding a way to serve the world that inspires remarkable and rewarding results. Service Above Self. (Once again, it all leads back to dear old Dad.)

There are three basic ingredients to the Personal Brand Echo. It starts with the Chi, the energy, which drives the act of extreme service, which usually results in delight on the part of the individual and the people who receive the service. Yes, there's a formula for it, but this is the last one. I promise!

$$E \Rightarrow ES \Rightarrow D$$

E (Life force or Energy or Chi) [leads to...]
Extreme Service [which leads to..]
Delight

A wise woman once told me that life is made up of the chances we take, and the promises we make, and how we measure up to both.

Canadian poet Robert Service quipped that "a promise made is a debt unpaid," and the most popular American poet of the twentieth century, Robert Frost wrote the surreal line, "The woods are lovely, dark and deep. But I have promises to keep" in his iconic poem about stopping by the woods on a snowy evening. Promises are large. They matter. They are not to be ignored.

But the most impactful lives are driven by more than promises. They are driven by individuals who have tapped into a deeper source than themselves and who channel that vibrant energy to deliver extreme service (within the industry or niche they know best) to render delight for a (usually) small or select audience.

They have flipped the focus, brought the fix and shrunk the audience.

Have you considered what lasting impact or delight you will have on the world? Have you considered what people will say in your eulogy?

Steven Covey includes an interesting exercise in his book *The Seven Habits of Highly Effective People*. He begins chapter two by painting a picture of someone going to a funeral service at a church. The reader soon discovers, oddly, that it is his or her own funeral.

Covey asks the reader to imagine four speakers, one from the family, another from work, a third who is a friend, and the fourth from a civic organization. What might each speaker say? What would you want each one to say about the life you lived? Get that mental image, Covey says, and work backwards from it until you reach today. Habit number two, accordingly, is "Begin with the end in mind."

Build your Personal Brand Echo the same way: begin with the end in mind, and never doubt the power of a personal brand.

145

ROSE THE RESILIENT

Rose was a Dutch Jew who somehow survived Auschwitz, although almost no one else in her family did. At the end of the war, she went home, where she met Luis Van Thyn, another Auschwitz survivor in Amsterdam. They married, immigrated to the U.S., settled in Shreveport, Louisiana, built a successful life, and raised a family, but Rose was unable to break free from the overwhelming guilt and sorrow of having survived the concentration camp when her parents and siblings did not. Depression plagued her for years, until she started making speeches.

Factoid: **Auschwitz concentration camp** *was a network of concentration and extermination camps built and operated by the Third Reich in Polish areas annexed by Nazi Germany during World War II. The camp's first commandant, Rudolf Höss, testified after the war at the Nuremberg Trials that up to three million people had died there, a figure since revised to 1.3 million, around ninety percent of them Jews. [Source: Wikipedia]*

Rose, it turned out, was a gifted public speaker, and as an orator she found great purpose. She captivated audiences with her first-hand account of how, as a child, she experienced and survived the atrocities underway in Holland and Poland during the Holocaust.

Initially, Rose told her story to anyone who would listen. She spoke to civic groups, educational panels, high school students, editorial boards, college classes, moms, dads, kids, Bible study groups and Rotary Clubs. The list was long. She found true solace and release from her still-overwhelming grief decades later by becoming a voice for her family, her generation, and in effect for all Holocaust survivors—repeating the mantra of "Never again!"

This message has been a frequent refrain among WW2 Holocaust survivors, but it has had few spokespeople like Rose. Each time she told her story, the applause was so deafening that no one wanted to take the podium to follow her. She was highly regarded, and her story changed lives.

In the early 1990s, I was a reporter for the ABC affiliate in Shreveport, Louisiana. When the film *Schindler's List* launched in 1993, our news director wanted to ride the movie's popularity and promotional campaign as a vehicle to highlight World War II survivors in the Shreveport area. Of course, Rose Van Thyn was at the top of the list of those we wanted to interview.

By this time, she was a regional celebrity with a following across northwest Louisiana and a strong reputation of poise, purpose, and passion. The TV station sent four of us, the Van Thyns, a videographer, and me, to Washington, D.C. to tour that city's new Holocaust museum. We produced a three-part series on the Van Thyns and their Holocaust experience.

For me, this experience was life altering. Rose gave me an education. I gave her, in my capacity as a reporter, a platform from which to tell her story to her broadest audience.

Rose didn't care a dime about raising money. In fact, she was rarely paid to speak. Instead, she tapped a much bigger cause that represented her extended family, cultural heritage, and world history. She raised awareness with a compelling autobiographical story that educated and even transformed people.

She often empowered her audiences to expect more and tolerate less. To lower the bar, as it were, on the degree of injustice each person should be willing to accept and what each would actively oppose. She encouraged everyone to tolerate less and speak out more.

You may not have a story like Rose. Few of us do. But we all make an impact on the people around us. We all leave a lasting impression on the family, neighbors, friends, and colleagues at work we see most frequently. We all have personal Brand Echoes.

Have you considered yours? What is its source? What drives you? How do the people in your inner circle regard you? Do you have an impact at all? Is it one of inspiration, motivation, encouragement, persistence, compassion, humor, and insight? Or is it one of criticism, gloom, negativity, insecurity, doubt, and abrasiveness?

Have you ever delivered what anyone would describe as 'extreme service'? If not, could you? What would that look like? Have you ever inspired delight? If so, how could you do it again?

The answer is important, because your Personal Brand Echo is the media platform that sets the stage for all the other messages you have to convey, including, ultimately, the message that drives your business success and your legacy.

If you are a person of purpose and passion, you will gravitate toward work that affords you the opportunity, and encourages you to exercise that purpose. Indeed, your Personal Brand Echo, for better or worse, animates and amplifies your workplace. Companies that summon purpose and passion are more productive, and in the end they outperform their competitors.

Another important (and distinctly democratic) point: you shouldn't be concerned about appealing to everyone. Not everyone will agree with your point or passion or perhaps even your "Chi." That's all right.

Asserting one position often means having to disavow something else. Don't fret over the few who believe differently or have a different approach. More will usually respect you for speaking *your* truth and carving out *your* brand identity.

THE POWER OF ONE

I'm not the only one arguing this point, by the way. Back in 1997, Tom Peters wrote an article for *Fast Company* magazine titled "The Brand Called You." In it, he said, "We are CEOs of our own companies: Me, Inc. To be in business today, your most important job is to be head marketer for the brand called You."

In 2009, Peter Montoya wrote a book also called The Brand Called You. *In it, he asserted, "A personal brand creates expectations in the minds of others of what they'll get when they work with you."*

It's time to reconsider that concept. Not just for the moment, or the transaction, or even the business being built, but for the life being lived and the surrounding lives being impacted every day.

In his 2009 book GSD&M, *CEO and fellow Texan Roy Spence drives home the same point regarding the fuel that drives great individuals and great companies. He says, "Having clarity about the ultimate purpose of the time and energy you spend doing what you do is the cornerstone of a culture of purpose. It's what drives everything you do. It's your reason for being that goes beyond making money, yet it almost always results in making more money than you ever thought possible. If you have a purpose and can articulate it with clarity and passion, then everything makes sense and everything flows. You feel good about what you're doing and clear about how to get there. You're excited to get up in the mornings and you sleep easier at night."*

I couldn't agree more. After all, I saw this over and over during my career as a journalist—the passion that drives great performance and leaves behind a tremendous Personal Brand Echo.

That's why the tighter the alignment between the Personal Brand Echo and the Commercial Brand Echo, the better. The individual who is closely matched with his or her passion is much

> A Personal Brand Echo is important because it serves the immediate community in a way that produces a profound and lasting effect.

more effective, much more harmonious, and ultimately much more fulfilled.

The objective of *Brand Echonomics* is effective communication, not specifically leadership, but it turns out that powerful leaders are almost always powerful communicators. Powerful communicators, in turn, almost always have resilient Brand Echoes. Their words and passions live after them.

So, your Personal Brand Echo isn't quite as dependent on the specific service you deliver as it is on the *passion* (Chi) you exert, the deep, intrinsic *value* you deliver, and the ultimate *delight* you render.

Maximize your Chi.

FOR DISCUSSION

What is your Chi?

What is that cause—bigger than yourself—to which you are committed?

How can you incorporate it into your life so that it inspires your PBE?

How does it align with your business Brand Echo?

THE FISHBOWL FACTOR

Managing Your 360 Degree Brand Echo

> No Brand Echo can exist in isolation. Your Brand Echo, whether personal or commercial, exists in a 360-degree environment of public scrutiny. Seek close alignment between your personal and commercial Brand Echoes, alignment *of* and *on* purpose.

One more secret: There is no more privacy. The more success and notoriety you attain, the more closely your professional AND PERSONAL Brand Echoes will be scrutinized. There is almost no way to separate them.

C all them the Bull and the Eagle.

In October of 1984, the Army's former chief of staff filed a 120-million-dollar defamation lawsuit against CBS News and 60 Minutes reporter Mike Wallace.

The issue? In a 1982 documentary, CBS asserted that General William Westmoreland manipulated information during the Vietnam War to deceive President Lyndon B. Johnson and sway public opinion.

A key point in the case was that Westmoreland, like any public figure, needed to prove something called "actual malice" on the part of CBS. In other words, to win, he needed to prove that CBS acted with knowledge and/or reckless disregard of the falsehood.

I remember this case distinctly because of its prominent media coverage while I was in college. My fellow students and the faculty discussed it at length. Westmoreland was the "Bull" of the Army, a Pentagon leader, a distinguished combat veteran and former commandant at West Point.

Mike Wallace was considered by some to be the "Eagle" of American investigative journalism, exposing the sinister and the corrupt, although some of my classmates considered him much more of a "Viper" for castigating a decorated war hero. They asked, shouldn't the media have more respect for a man who had a distinguished career serving in the armed forces? Shouldn't it be a simple matter of fact or fiction? Shouldn't Westmoreland be entitled to the same rights against libel and slander?

Well, no.

People in the public eye are inherently subject to more scrutiny and less privacy. They live in a veritable fishbowl. In legal proceedings, public officials and celebrities must meet a higher standard in order to prove libel. The premise is that individuals who voluntarily submit themselves to public scrutiny can reasonably expect a lower degree of privacy than ordinary citizens. Westmoreland definitely fit the description.

Today, the same is true in court for Justin Beiber, Tiger Woods and Michael Dell.

Public figures just don't get much protection against scrutiny and critique.

WE'RE ALL PUBLIC FIGURES TODAY

According to U.S. civil law, a public figure is someone who has voluntarily stepped into the public eye despite the public scrutiny associated with his or her profession. This happens when someone runs for office, becomes a CEO of a large corporation, performs in movies or onstage, records popular music, or becomes a TV news anchor. Consider Al Gore, Bill Gates, Julia Roberts, Diane Sawyer, and Lady Gaga.

But here's the point: Very few of us can expect complete privacy anymore, regardless of our professions. As a former Army Chief of Staff, Westmoreland couldn't expect it in 1984, Donald Trump can't expect it now, and neither can we. Today, our lives are digitized and publicized more than ever, whether you're an Army general, a network news reporter, head of a company, or even an entrepreneur.

Think about it. Anyone who voluntarily creates a public Facebook profile or uploads a video to YouTube can expect a global audience. Anyone who shows up in a two-minute segment on a local newscast can expect that digital clip to be archived for decades, and everyone who flies can plan to be inspected for weapons in the most private of places. At every bank and every ATM, we are on camera and every credit card swipe creates a digital profile. And on and on.

In the terms of the popular Fox series, 24, each of us is "on the grid" by virtue of our complicit participation in common twenty-first-century culture. We are each subject to profound scrutiny—unlike any other generation—whether in public or not, whether on stage or not, and whether at work or not.

Legally, yes, there is still a distinction between public and private citizens in court—if a libel or slander case goes to trial. My point is that—as a result of twenty-first-century culture—we are all living in a virtual fishbowl.

Brands exist "on the grid" as well. They are very much in the public eye and subject to constant scrutiny from all sides. You simply can't expect to build a "public" persona with a prodigious advertising or PR campaign, while keeping certain dimensions of it in private. Even people who have lived their entire lives outside any limelight are often subject to a level of observation and scrutiny unimagined by previous generations. One accidental posting, and your personal brand is likely to be fodder for the evening news.

I got used to this kind of scrutiny at an early age. I grew up as a fourth-generation Brady in the same Central Texas town where my great grandfather had been city marshal. So I was often reminded by my dad that certain behavioral standards were expected of me. He wanted me to honor my family's reputation and help protect it. Consequently, every time I left to meet up with friends or go on a date, my dad's parting words were, "Remember who you are!"

We all should.

I guess I didn't think about the deeper meaning of that edict at the time, but I sure do now. It was a summons to greatness, a reminder that I was part of a bigger family tableau—larger family brand and a Brady Family tapestry. My every action had a ripple effect far beyond the moment. My dad was concerned even then about a Personal Brand Echo. He knew it would last.

Because you too will be scrutinized from all angles, it's worth considering and protecting your Personal Brand Echo from all perspectives. The fact is, people today will develop an impression of you that transcends your professional role, title, and salary. Today, your Personal Brand Echo may also include your academic degree, social media profiles, family pedigree, home, health, hobbies, neighborhood activities, political involvement, children, and yes, your pets.

We live in a transparent culture. The Brand Echo, whether personal or professional, is now subject to scrutiny from every side. It must be a healthy, transparent 360-degree Brand Echo to survive. It must be respectable in every respect, not perfect or invincible, but good, decent, and honorable. Don't fool yourself into thinking you can hide part of your identity behind a veil of privacy. It rarely lasts. And the loftier the position to which you aspire, the closer the scrutiny.

If you really don't think these issues matter, you're not paying attention (cardinal sin Number One for a Brand Echo architect). Witness the stumble and collapse of one politician, A-list actor, minister, or CEO after another—when private personal train wrecks are made public.

THE LINK TO CORPORATE SOCIAL RESPONSIBILITY

If the concept of a 360-degree Brand Echo sounds similar to the concept of Corporate Social Responsibility, or CSR, that's because they're closely related. We do have an obligation to be good citizens and thoughtful caretakers. Yes, you may be talented at producing an amazing product or service, but are you a good steward of your resources? Do you treat your vendors well? What are the working conditions in your overseas factories? Do you pay your taxes? A glaring deficiency in one area can erode the good work done in another.

"Every time we've made a decision to do the right thing," says Patagonia founder Yvon Chouinard, "it ends up being good business." The company earned $500 million in gross 2011 sales, growing almost thirty percent in each of the past two years—all while setting the bar for sustainability. [Source: *Fast Company* March 2012]

Umair Haque is director of Havas Media Labs, a blogger for *Harvard Business Review*, and the author of *The New Capitalist Manifesto: Building a Disruptively Better Business*. Thinkers50 ranks him one of the world's most influential management gurus.

Haque makes the argument that companies must evolve their purpose from greatness in business to doing good in the larger global community. Regarding Pepsi, he says this:

"Pepsi, for example, is a 'great' company. It's great at mass-producing, push-distributing, mega-marketing, and hard-selling sugar water. But Pepsi is finding out the hard way that all of the above is a commodity.

"The shelves are brimming over with different flavors of sugary water—and the customers are tuning out, governments are attacking it, and rivals are bettering it. Pepsi's great at producing something that is bad for you; it isn't yet a company that maximizes good.

"Why did Pepsi strive to get 'more good' with radical initiatives like Refresh? Because in the twenty-first century, merely being great in the sugar water business is a one-way ticket to strategic irreverence and economic oblivion."

Your Corporate or Personal Brand Echo is a compilation of impressions that customers and vendors will develop from a variety of sources, not just your advertising PR or social media profile. The public is curious and clever, and it's all about who you are.

What I call the "Believability Factor" trumps almost everything else. As I mentioned earlier, we are a media-savvy, sophisticated, and in many ways cynical culture. Suspicions are usually high, and they get higher at the first whiff of falsehood. That's why the Personal Brand Echo can be one of the most powerful influencing factors in business today, and why it has the potential to build an empire. In many cases, it has.

Take John Deere. He built a better steel plow in 1837 in a small manufacturing shop in Illinois. Now the company employs more than fifty-five thousand people with annual revenue of $26 billion.

Take Mary Kay Ash. She started selling cosmetics with her son and a $5,000 personal investment in 1963. Now the company achieves more than $3 billion in annual global sales.

Take Walt Disney. A Missouri cartoonist moved to LA with his brother Roy to launch a small studio. Today, Disney, Inc. is the largest media conglomerate in the world based on revenue, with a Hollywood studio, numerous TV networks, and fourteen major theme parks around the world.

Personal Brand Echoes are powerful.

BRAND MANAGEMENT AT HOME AND BEYOND

As you may recall from Chapter One, I have a big wooden door hanging in my home office. It's about ten feet wide and five feet tall and is covered in cattle brands from ranches near my hometown of Georgetown, Texas. This door is more than a hundred years old.

I'm not a rancher, but I keep this door because it's a powerful reminder of my family history, our cultural history, and the importance of a brand. I keep it because of what it stands for—the power and reach of a substantive Brand Echo.

I predict the day is coming when families and other private entities will invest more in brand management. They will wonder, "What's the 'family brand'? What's our crest? Our motto? What does it represent? Are we living up to it?"

I believe we are at the dawn of a new era in which branding will reach beyond the commercial arena. Already, more industries, events, churches, nonprofits, families, and individuals want to invest in a distinctive brand, not a logo or a design or a motto, not an emblem burned into a wooden door, but a brand concept. And it will have to be a brand built with 360-degree transparency. It will have to be holistic and authentic, not just a good product or service, but emblematic of good people doing good work, living out their Chi and establishing an Echo that will reach far into the future.

As I've explained, the basis of the most effective brand concepts will be powerful messages. The messages that reach the furthest and best serve the needs of the people will generate a powerful Brand Echo because people will talk about them to their intimate circles of friend and family. The Brand Echo will outlast every other type of message.

How it's delivered will change, in part because the Brand Echo developed in the business arena cannot live in isolation. It will eventually (or immediately) be lumped together with your private, social, charitable, college football, vacation, and neighborhood cookout Brand Echo. We no longer have the ability to compartmentalize the message.

If you want to build a brand in the public arena, you no longer have the luxury of personal privacy. We are living in a "digital fishbowl," or an era of the 360 Degree Brand Echo. In other words, know that

> Brands are now scrutinized from all angles. They must represent the good and the great in every sector. There are no secrets.

when you let your hair down, you're still building a Brand Echo. And the higher your position, the less privacy you can expect.

FOR DISCUSSION

How does your PBE support and supplement your business Brand Echo?

What components of your life could work against the business Brand Echo you are trying to build?

CELEBRITY TO SERVANT

Beyond Marshall McLuhan: It's the Message, Not the Medium

> Brand Echonomics is really about adapting your mindset from personal gain to selfless service. Solve a key problem in a distinctive way, inspire a story, and make it easy for others to tell the story. Tap your Chi and your Brand Echo will travel far.

One final insight: Brand Echonomics is not a secret science. It's about personal AND professional growth and, ultimately, about building a message that matters. It's about finding meaning, and also about making meaning. Profit most by serving best.

In 1964, Canadian scholar and educator Marshall McLuhan taught us "the medium is the message." He coined the term in a groundbreaking book, *Understanding Media: The Exten-*

sions of Man, in which he asserted that modern mass media have a societal impact far beyond the specific messages or the content conveyed.

In that era, McLuhan was correct. Broadcast news—radio first, then TV—represented entirely new platforms to convey news and information to broad audiences. We learned differently and behaved differently because of it. Television news definitely trained us to digest video segments in a specific sequence of ninety-second stories with an introduction, conclusion, and overall flow delivered by a host.

Today, many argue that the internet is having an equally profound impact on society and possibly even the anatomy of the human brain.

Nicholas Carr argues that point in his 2011 book, The Shallows, *in which he states that the internet is chipping away at our societal capacity "for reason, perception, memory and emotion."*

Most neurologists would agree, as would many parents!

Conversely, a Brand Echo rises above the individual medium. It is inspirational, viral, and infectious, and it transcends the media on which it is conveyed. A Brand Echo travels on its own strength and relevance. Whether print, broadcast, digital, or even verbal, a Brand Echo reverberates and registers with customers, consumers, and ultimately with Catalysts on its own merit.

The message trumps the medium...if it's the *right* message. After all, some of the most profound life events happen in the most humble and unassuming of circumstances. Some of the most powerful messages you've ever received were very likely conveyed in private. And you'll never forget them. A vacant theater. A remote country beach. An empty sanctuary or a ballpark. A maternity ward. A hospice bed. I've seen the miraculous in many of these places, but one of the most moving and life-altering events of my life occurred in that tropical jungle on that border between Mexico and Guatemala.

I was transformed, in the wink of an eye, from a pompous and self-absorbed TV news announcer into an honest journalist. I was trans-figured from a guy who wanted to explore and even exploit a foreign crisis for his own professional gain to being a courier for a people who desperately wanted the world to know about their struggle.

Wayne Dyer describes similar life-changing transitions in his book The Shift *as personal, internal movements from entitlement to humility, or "...from Ambition to Meaning."*

That transformation gave me the opportunity to experience the amazing and untold circumstances of another group of people, to find the compelling story of value in their experiences, then to convey that message to a broad audience. An arrogant sense of entitlement became a humble sense of purpose. From pseudo-celebrity to servant, I was taught that lesson at gunpoint, and thankfully, it has lasted a lifetime.

THE MAGIC BULLET IS YOU

One last thing.

The most powerful Brand Echoes aren't developed by "tricking" the news media or by developing a funny but inauthentic ad campaign with a catchy slogan or a popular celebrity. Yes, I know my friends in the large agency industry still make millions with effective campaigns of this sort, but the tide is turning. From "push" messaging to "pull," we live in a new era of authenticity and transparency.

So first find that inner source of purpose that inspires you to serve people in a big, bold, even audacious way. Discover your

"Chi" or the "holy inspiration" that works through you to serve your clients in a bigger, better way. Ask yourself what it would look like, what it would sound like, what it would *feel* like to align your business with a deep calling, a life force that allows you to tap a higher energy.

Then, remember the three questions I shared to tap the Brand Echo:

1. Who are you (or—metaphorically—who is the client)?

2. Where are you going (or what problem is the client trying to solve)? What disruptive level of service can you offer within your industry to meet that need? Developing a core business concept that delivers real value to customers in an innovative, inclusive, and immediate way creates a powerful message.

3. Who is traveling with you (or what source of information is feeding the client, to whom does that client listen)?

Then foster a climate in which customers experience your value and share it. On the platform they choose. That's the essence of the Brand Echo. The magic bullet is *you*.

The most potent stories develop a life on their own, so have a better story to tell. If necessary, hire a journalist who's ready to help you tell a great story.

Or better yet, create an experience in which your Catalyst will have a great story to tell!

What unique, distinct, pertinent, relevant, valuable, and powerful message can you convey (or inspire) about your product or service? And yes, service is the key. Discover a way to serve more people doing what you most enjoy, and you will be more successful, happier, more fulfilled, and more aligned with your

Chi. How can you deliver something remarkable, then inspire your Catalyst to go to work telling your story?

Remember the formula: (C + P + Y = Story) x Ct = Brand Echo.

Serve the customer better than your competitor does. Make a difference.

Shrink the audience to create a phenomenal experience. Create an experience that inspires the Catalyst to tell an

> Transform yourself and create a Brand Echo with a powerful message of service that will last a lifetime...and beyond.

amazing story. Then you can reach an enormous audience with a powerful Brand Echo.

Keep in mind, also, that your singular Brand Echo does not have to be stagnant. The central brand message can and often should evolve, especially as your central company or organization churns out more products and services. Consider Tide, Gatorade, GE, and other major retailers. The core message remains consistent, but the products, the pitches, the stories, and even the Echoes evolve.

Find a way to be a servant, in a unique and powerful way, and then do it often enough to surprise and delight your customers. This will generate a great story. If you can do this, you'll have a Brand Echo that travels far and wide. Possibly more than one.

The final and most important question in this book is this: *What is the Brand Echo you would like your grandchildren to tell their children about you many years from now?*

In other words, what is the impact you would like to have that will outlast the individual business transactions, the individual business, or the individual life? What can you do to be of the greatest service to your customers and clients so that it will astonish them and trigger a Brand Echo—your Brand Echo—that will last for generations?

FOR DISCUSSION: THINK BACK

Have you had a mountaintop transformation of your own that has changed your life for the better?

How did it inspire you?

If not, what might such a transformation entail, and how might your life change as a result?

BIG SECRETS

1. Most brands are invisible.

2. Brand Echonomics goes BEYOND the promise. A Brand Echo is a pledge.

3. "He profits most who serves best."

4. You're NOT the most important brand messenger regarding your product or service. Neither is your CMO or ad agency. Your satisfied customer is.

5. Media fatigue means it is more difficult now than ever to deliver the right brand message to the right audience. Fewer people are paying attention.

6. Scientifically, stories sell. They are the key to getting an audience to listen, learn and remember.

7. Every successful story follows an ancient formula.

8. Pay attention. Listen to the customer, learn and earn.

9. Once you understand the client, you need to understand what drives her.

10. The key to developing a great Brand Echo is not a better storytelling technique or technology, it's simply a better story.

11. We are a nation of tribes. Learn the language of the tribe you're trying to reach.

12. You can start the Brand Echo by spending less.

13. The era of "push" media is fading; "pull" media is on the rise. That is, attract an audience, don't assault one!

14. Social media is social. Consider it a party. Be present. Be authentic (don't outsource). Serve others. Don't brag. Be gracious.

15. A compelling story sells itself. Journalists want to cover TOPICS, not produce commercials for your product or service!

16. Advertising is losing its effectiveness, yet still it survives. Use it for awareness only. Find a way to TARGET all ads. Generic campaigns waste enormous budgets.

17. A Brand Echo is about more than making money. It's about meaning, relevance, and EARNING attention, not buying it. Create messages that matter.

18. Personal Brand Echoes mean more and last longer than commercial Brand Echoes.

19. There is no more privacy. The more success and notoriety you attain, the more closely your professional AND PERSONAL Brand Echoes will be scrutinized. There is almost no way to separate them.

20. Brand Echonomics is not a secret science. It's about personal AND professional growth and, ultimately, about building a message that matters to others. It's about finding meaning, and also about making meaning. And your Echo will carry far and wide. Profit most by serving best.

SUGGESTED READINGS

It's Not What You Sell, It's What You Stand For by Roy Spence

Start with Why by Simon Sinek

Whole New Mind by Dan Pink

The Experience Economy by Joseph Pine II and James H. Gilmore

The Purple Cow by Seth Godin

Linchpin by Seth Godin

The Hero with a Thousand Faces by Joseph Campbell

Made to Stick by Chip Heath and Dan Heath

The Shift by Dr. Wayne Dyer

The Seven Habits of Highly Effective People by Steven R. Covey

The Tipping Point by Malcolm Gladwell

The New Rules of Marketing and PR by David Meerman Scott

The Brand Called You by Peter Montoya

The Capitalist Manifesto by Umair Haque

Freakonomics by Steven D. Levitt and Stephen J. Dubner

The Shallows by Nicholas Carr

The Rise of the Creative Class by Richard Florida

ABOUT THE AUTHOR

Jeff Brady is an award-winning journalist, news anchor, talk show host, and entrepreneur. He is the CEO of Brady Media Group, a Dallas-based Brand Strategy, PR, and Content Marketing firm. He also hosts The Texas Daily, a one-hour TV news and talk show in the nation's fifth-largest media market. He spent almost twenty years in TV newsrooms across the southwestern U.S. For nearly a decade, Jeff anchored the news at WFAA-TV in Dallas-Ft. Worth.

Prior to Dallas, Jeff served as the primary male anchor at KSAT-TV in San Antonio. Earlier, he worked for TV newsrooms in Louisiana and in Arizona.

Before his civilian life, Jeff served as an officer in the U.S. Marine Corps during the Persian Gulf War, stationed in Saudi Arabia for Operations Desert Shield and Desert Storm.

He now lives in Dallas with his wife Wesley and their three children.

INDEX

NOTES

NOTES

NOTES